Hikernut's

Canyon Companion

A Guide to the Best Canyon Hikes in the American Southwest

Brian J. Lane

©2013 by

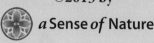

a Sense *of* Nature

Edited by Kathleen Bryant

Text, photographs, photo illustrations, maps,
graphics, and book design by Brian J. Lane
(unless otherwise specified).

All rights reserved. No part of this book may be reproduced in any form or
by any electronic or mechanical means including information storage and re-
trieval systems without permission in writing from the publisher, except by a
reviewer, who may quote brief passages.

NOTE: The author assumes no liability for any injury or damages resulting
from the use of information contained herein. The maps provided in this
guide are for illustrative purposes only. They are not to scale and are not intended for use in route finding. Each has been hand drawn, and may be subject
to inconsistencies. A detailed topographic map of the area is necessary for
hiking and backpacking.

FIRST EDITION

ISBN-13: 978-1-58157-164-6
Library of Congress Control Number:

Published by The Countryman Press,
P.O. Box 748, Woodstock, VT 05091

Distributed by W.W. Norton & Company, Inc.,
500 Fifth Avenue, New York, NY 10110

Printed in the United States of America

10 9 8 7 6 5 4 3 2 1

Also by The Countryman Press and Brian J. Lane:
Hikernut's Grand Canyon Companion –
A Guide to Hiking and Backpacking the Most Popular Trails into the Canyon:
Bright Angel, South Kaibab, and North Kaibab Trails

"*Hikernut*" is a registered trademark of Brian J. Lane and A Sense of Nature, LLC

Background photo: Rock formations along Burr Trail Road, Grand Staircase-Escalante Nat'l Monument.
Front cover photo: Fifty-Foot Falls and cascades, Havasu Canyon.
Back cover photo of the author by John Ducasse.

About the Author

Born and raised in North Brookfield, Massachusetts, I've lived in Arizona since the early 1990s. My wife La Quita and I have a small ranch near Sedona, where we raise our animals and grow veggies. A former U.S. Marine, and a NOLS/WMI certified Wilderness First Responder, I've attended Clark University, Massachusetts College of Art, and Kaplan University, majoring in art, media, and paralegal studies, among others. I am also a horticulturist, forestry and wildlife conservationist, and a master watershed steward advocating for watershed ecosystems and sustainable resource management.

Author Brian Lane inside Buckskin Gulch
(Photo by Nina Rehfeld)

As for the "Hikernut" moniker, I've been using it since the first time I signed up for an email account many years ago. I figured that giving myself such an address would help ensure that I continued to get out there and keep hiking. The nickname also came about due to the so-called "crazy" pace I tend to keep when hiking uphill. The "hikernut" sobriquet can be defined simply as another term for a hiking enthusiast. So take heart, guys; it is not a medical condition.

I hike these canyons to experience their incomparable scenery and solitude, for the challenge of hiking such rugged areas, and as a test of my fitness. Hiking calls me to get outside, stay fit, and physically push myself. I believe those who don't test themselves—exerting past the point of physical discomfort—will never really know themselves.

Hike safe and have fun!
Brian J. Lane
Sedona, Arizona

This book is dedicated to the people and organizations working diligently to protect this special region, including the Grand Canyon Trust, Southern Utah Wilderness Alliance, Sierra Club, Center for Biological Diversity, and the Natural Resources Defense Council, among others. Additional thanks goes out to all the National Park, Bureau of Land Management, and Forest Service rangers, employees, and volunteers helping to make the most of our outdoor experience while also preserving the land within their jurisdictions for generations to come.

Further dedication once again goes out to my dearest hiking and life companion, my wife La Quita, for all her patience, input, and support, and to Mom, Dad, Sue, Rob, and the rest of our family; we love you. Thanks too for all my canyon country hiking partners and the cherished memories they helped create, including John Ducasse, Mike Hubacz, Joanna Hubacz, Tom Hubacz, David Woods, Glenn Southworth, Ron Chambers, Danny Sanderson, Beth-ellen Zang, Nina Rehfeld, and Larry Lindahl. And a big thank you to Kathleen Bryant for her excellent editing skills and other assistance with this book.

Photo: La Quita Lane standing in the opening of Pine Tree Arch, Arches National Park

Table of Contents

People need wild places. Whether or not we think we do, we do. We need to be able to taste grace and know again that we desire it. We need to experience a landscape that is timeless, whose agenda moves at the pace of speciation and glaciers. To be surrounded by a singing, mating, howling commotion of other species, all of which love their lives as much as we do ours, and none of which could possibly care less about us in our place. It reminds us that our plans are small and somewhat absurd. It reminds us why, in those cases in which our plans might influence many future generations, we ought to choose carefully. Looking out on a clean plank of planet earth, we can get shaken right down to the bone by the bronze-eyed possibility of lives that are not our own.

Barbara Kingsolver

Always in big woods (or canyons), when you leave familiar ground and step off alone to a new place, there will be, along with feelings of curiosity and excitement, a little nagging of dread. It is the ancient fear of the unknown, and it is your bond with the wilderness you are going into. What you are doing is exploring. You are understanding the first experience, not of the place, but of yourself in that place. It is the experience of our essential loneliness, for nobody can discover the world for anybody else. It is only after we have discovered it for ourselves that it becomes common ground, and a common bond, and we cease to be alone.

Wendell Berry

**Adventure is not in the guidebook
and beauty is not on the map.
Seek and ye shall find.**

Terry and Renny Russell

Chapter One

Introduction

The trails of the world be
countless, and most of
the trails be tried;
You tread on the heels of
the many, 'til you come
where the ways divide;
And one lies safe in the
sunlight, and the other is
dreary and wan,
Yet you look aslant at the
Lone Trail, and the Lone
Trail lures you on.

Robert Service

Amazing, unadulterated natural beauty. That is the essence of what the picturesque Southwestern United States has to offer. This gorgeous region delivers an abundance of huge, open, deep blue skies, in a sun-filled, warm, dry climate, relatively free of the humidity and biting insects so familiar to those who live in so many other areas of this splendid country. It rewards those who seek with delightful sunrises and incredible sunsets. It is a visual paradise full of multicolored, layered, sculpted, and folded rock. It is harsh desert, filled with dry, rocky, and sand-choked creek beds, ephemeral pools, and one immense preponderant river—the awesome Colorado. The Southwest has an inherent innate majesty whose magnificence must be experienced to be appreciated, and unless your spirit is numb, the explorations included in this book will move your soul.

Spider Rock, Canyon de Chelly National Monument

Side Step: Time Zones

Most of the State of Arizona does not observe Daylight Saving Time (the Navajo Nation being the exception). Therefore, its time changes from Mountain Standard Time between November and March to align with Pacific Daylight Time from March through November. Remember when traveling between Utah and Arizona during the warmer months (March though November) that you will change time zones and Utah will be an hour ahead of Arizona time.

Sheer-walled canyons, expansive grasslands, red buttes, and arches, lots of arches, the Colorado Plateau contains some of the most spectacular scenery in the world, attracting nature-loving visitors seeking its open vistas and wild beauty. The canyon lands of the Southwest are beautiful, numerous, sometimes dangerous, and most of all—alluring. Where I live, in Sedona, Arizona, even on my worst days, I always find something soothing about the cottony white clouds, endless cerulean blue sky, and towering red rocks—it calms me to the marrow.

I have lived in and hiked around the Southwest for over twenty years now, and in this book I'll try to describe a few of the preeminent hikes found in this diverse and remote area. The trails I have included in this guide are the cream of the crop, the trails that most epitomize the Southwest canyon lands. If you wish to really explore this area, I would label these hikes the "essentials."

These journeys will bring you to some of the most diverse landscapes on earth, including open vistas, slot canyons, dry deserts, riparian creeks, and emerald forests. At times you'll be hiking in sand, on slickrock, or sloshing around in a stream or creek. Some of the trails listed here are easy day hikes and some are very strenuous overnight backpack trips, but none would be considered technical canyoneering or climbing excursions. In other words, these trails run the gamut, but they require no special skills (besides basic land navigation and wilderness skills), and they are all worth your time and effort. Each excursion is spectacular in its own right.

All hikes take place within the distinct physiographic province known as the Colorado Plateau. Covering some 130,000 square miles, this magnificent land area is actually a large basin encircled by highlands and permeated with numerous plateaus. Made up largely of deserts interspersed with forests, the plateau is a geological wonderland of brightly colored rock perpetually eroded and sculpted into various eccentric shapes referred to by such unusual terms as hoodoos, arches, goblins, narrows, fins, bridges, reefs, and slots.

The Colorado Plateau is bounded on all sides by major geological features, including Utah's Uinta Range to the north, Nevada's Great Basin to the west, the Colorado Rockies to the east, and the Mogollon Rim of Arizona to the south. Volcanic activity also formed a few smaller, more intimate mountain clusters scattered around the plateau, such as the Henry Mountains, the La Sals, the Abajos, and the San Francisco Peaks, rising prominently along the varied horizons of canyon country. The plateau is a giant drainage basin with ninety percent of its excess precipitation being carried off by the ubiquitous Colorado River and its other major tributaries, the Green, the San Juan, and the Little Colorado rivers.

Elevations along the Colorado Plateau range from a high of nearly 13,000 feet, down to the 2,400 foot level. Although a semiarid environment prevails in this region, the variety of ecosystems ranges from high alpine conditions to desert sage. The dominant Sierra Nevada Mountains to the west preclude moisture-laden clouds from reaching the Southwest; as a result of this rainshadow effect, the annual precipitation averages only about ten to twelve inches each year.

A huge amount of the plateau consists of protected public lands, and includes nine national parks, one national historic park, sixteen national monuments, dozens of wilderness areas, and other state and federal recreational areas. This region has the highest concentration of park lands on the continent. Although rich in natural resources and always at risk for over-exploitation, the plateau's greatest financial and commercial asset is the fantastic natural landscape itself, and the related tourism that comes with such overwhelming scenic appeal.

Tonto Trail with Granite Rapids in the distance, Grand Canyon National Park

You have traveled too fast over false ground;
Now your soul has come to take you back.

Take refuge in your senses, open up
To all the small miracles you rushed through.

Become inclined to watch the way of the rain
When it falls slow and free.

Imitate the habit of twilight,
Taking time to open the well of color
That fostered the brightness of day.

Draw alongside the silence of stone
Until its calmness can claim you.

John O'Donohue

The hiker can go without combing his hair or shaving and will be accepted as perfectly normal. He can get dirty and his friends will speak to him jovially. His clothes may be in tatters, and people will think nothing of it. If there happens to be a little rock dust on his shirt or trousers, or if his clothes are a trifle torn, so much the better. Of such stuff are hiking heroes made. The hiker doesn't have to talk very much, say witty things, hold a glass in his hands, or laugh lightly at banalities. His is a world of opposites, and no one cares or worries about it.

Ann Sutton

Beware though: hiking in the southwest can be challenging on many levels. The dry heat so comforting in spring and fall can quickly turn dangerous during the extreme heat of summer. Those accustomed to hiking along a sharply delineated trail meandering through a green forest can easily miss a turn and get lost when hiking along an open slickrock expanse or in a canyon wash when the trail suddenly scrambles out of the dry creek bed. Climbing out of some canyons can seem relentless while muscles are cramping. Cactus can be unforgiving; scorpions and rattle snakes can, and do, sting and bite. Storms many miles away can trigger killing flash floods while you are totally unaware of the threat headed your way, and backcountry water sources may dry out completely.

"Whoa," you say, "I just wanted to explore some beautiful Southwest canyons!" None of these things will probably ever happen to you, as long as you take care and plan properly. That's what this book is really all about, trying to keep you safe and informed while you bask in the joy of hiking and exploring this overwhelmingly wondrous region.

All information contained in this book is based on my own particular (some could say peculiar?) hiking and backpacking experiences and other techniques I have learned over the years. I do not assume responsibility for any injury or damages resulting from the use of information provided herein. More importantly, all information provided in this book is subject to change. Each park or recreational area has its own specific system concerning permits, and these procedures seem to change almost annually. Medical and nutritional advice can change as new science evolves, trails and roads can flood or wash out completely during severe storms, and public transportation systems always appear to be in a state of flux. The rocks may not change for lifetimes to come, but most everything else, it seems, is of a metamorphic nature. I will provide updates and corrections to this publication as feasible, but anyone entering into the backcountry and taking on such endeavors is responsible for his or her own safety. Make sure you contact the overseeing agency for any region you are planning to explore for important updates before you enter the wilderness.

Whew! Now, let's get started planning your trip with a map of the region followed by the ten most essential items everyone should carry while day hiking and exploring in canyon country, plus a more extensive backpacking list.

The Canyon Lands of the Colorado Plateau

⭐1 *Antelope Canyon* Navajo Tribal Park

⭐2 *Buckskin Gulch* Paria Canyon–Vermilion Cliffs NM

⭐3 *Coyote Gulch* Glen Canyon NRA

⭐4 *Devils Garden Primitive Loop* Arches NP

⭐5 *Druid Arch* Canyonlands NP

⭐6 *Havasu Canyon* Havasupai Tribal Lands

⭐7 *Hermit Trail* Grand Canyon NP

⭐8 *The Narrows* Zion NP

⭐9 *Navajo/Peekaboo/Queen's Garden* Bryce Canyon NP

⭐10 *Upper Muley Twist Canyon* Capitol Reef NP

⭐11 *West Fork Oak Creek* Coconino National Forest

⭐12 *White House Ruins* Canyon de Chelly NM

1 Aztec Ruins NM
2 Black Canyon/Gunnison NP
3 Cedar Breaks NM
4 Chaco Culture NHP
5 Colorado NM
6 Curecanti NM
7 Canyons of the Ancients NM
8 Dinosaur NM
9 El Malpais NM
10 El Morro NM
11 Grand Canyon–Parashant NM
12 Grand Staircase–Escalante NM
13 Hovenweep NM
14 Hubbell Trading Post NHS
15 Lake Mead NRA
16 Mesa Verde NP
17 Montezuma Castle NM
18 Monument Valley NTP
19 Natural Bridges NM
20 Navajo NM
21 Petrified Forest NP
22 Petroglyph NM
23 Pipe Spring NM
24 Rainbow Bridge NM
25 Sunset Crater Volcano NM
26 Tuzigoot NM
27 Walnut Canyon NM
28 Wupatki NM

1 Uinta Mtns
2 La Sal Mtns
3 Fishlake Mtns
4 Henry Mtns
5 Abajo Mtns
6 Navajo Mtn
7 Carrizo Mtns
8 San Juan Mtns
9 San Francisco Peaks
10 Zuni Mtns
11 San Mateo Mtns
12 White Mtns

The Ten Essentials

✿ **Water**: I take a minimum of one quart for every hour of hiking, keeping a sport drink mixture with electrolytes in at least one bottle. You'll need more going uphill—and even more in the summer. Make sure you take long drinks, not small sips, allowing the water to hydrate the body and not just wet the mouth.

✿ **Sun protection**: Hat, sunglasses, sunscreen, lip balm

✿ **Map, compass, and trail description**: Know the basics of land navigation.

✿ **First-aid kit**: Be sure to include blister treatments and ibuprofen for the body's aches and pains.

✿ **Extra food**: I take mostly energy bars and trail mix for the trail and dehydrated meals for camp.

✿ **Flashlight or headlamp**

✿ **Small repair kit**: Light wire, duct tape, sewing kit

✿ **Extra clothing**: Something to keep you warm and dry if you need to spend the night.

✿ **Lighter or fire starter**

✿ **Emergency shelter**: Rain poncho or reflective blanket

The Backpacking List

⛰ **Food and Water**

✿ **Water bottles**: I usually take 2 one-liter bottles, one with plain water and another with a sport drink mixture. For overnight trips I also carry a collapsible canteen for camp and have a large capacity water bladder inside my backpack.

✿ **Water purification**: This includes filters, chemical treatments, UV treatments, or other water treatment systems.

✿ **Food**: About two pounds per day for each person

✿ **Backpack stove**: Lightweight canister type

✿ **Cooking pot with cover**: Titanium is really light—but expensive.

✿ **Fork and spoon (or spork)**: Plastic or titanium

✿ **Trash bag**: A large sealable plastic bag will usually do.

✿ **Drinking cup**

⛰ **Shelter**

✿ **Tent or bivy shelter**: Quality and lightweight—no more than about six pounds for a two-person tent.

✿ **Sleeping bag**: Temperature rated to match your hiking season and climate

✿ **Sleeping pad**: Self-inflating, foam, or air mattress

List

≋ Clothing
✪ **Hiking boots**: Lightweight, with good ankle protection, and well broken-in
✪ **Socks**: I wear a thin synthetic liner sock with a heavier wool or synthetic outer sock.
✪ **Hat**: Wide-brimmed for sun protection
✪ **Shirt and pants**: Lightweight, comfortable layers, appropriate to the season (fleece for cool weather and cotton for the summer heat)
✪ **Underwear**: Comfortable, preferably synthetic or silk during the day and cotton for sleeping
✪ **Insulated jacket**: Poly-filled, down, or fleece
✪ **Off-trail shoes**: Sandals or other lightweight slip-ons for off-trail comfort
✪ **Rain coat or poncho**
✪ **Gloves**

≋ Hygiene
✪ **Human waste disposal bag** (if required) and toilet paper
✪ **Anti-bacterial hand sanitizer** and/or biodegradable soap, anti-bacterial wipes
✪ **Toothbrush and toothpaste**
✪ **Small lightweight towel**

≋ Emergency
✪ **First-aid kit**: A good comprehensive kit that includes a basic first-aid book. If you or anyone else in your group is allergic to insect bites, the kit should include an EpiPen, and everyone should know how to use it.
✪ **Repair kit**: Duct tape, plastic ties, light wire, nylon twine, nylon repair kit, sewing kit, and safety pins. Leatherman and Buck both make handy miniature multi-tools.
✪ **Signal device**: I carry a tin camping mirror.
✪ **Fire Starter**: Waterproof matches or lighter

≋ Miscellaneous
✪ **20 feet of light rope**: To hang your food bag
✪ **Bug repellent**: Be sure to keep DEET off your skin and Gore-Tex type fabrics.
✪ **Small pocketknife**
✪ **Watch or timepiece**
✪ **Extra batteries**
✪ **Pen, pencil, and paper** (for notes and sketches)

≋ Optional
✪ **Hiking sticks**: They give you stability and literally take tons of weight from your knees and ankles.
✪ **Pillow**: Small stuff sack, or inflatable
✪ **Camera**: Include extra memory cards or film
✪ **Rain pants and pack cover**

Chapter Two

Trails & Maps

After walking for days, coming home bugbitten, shins bruised, nose peeling, feet and hands swollen, I feel ablaze with life. I suspect that the canyons give me an intensified sense of living partly because I not only face the basics of living and survival, but carry them on my back. And in my head. And this intense personal responsibility gives me an overwhelming sense of freedom I know nowhere else.

Ann Zwinger

Here they are, the top twelve canyon hikes in the American Southwest. These are, of course, my own personal choices subjectively shaped by experience and therefore open to debate. While I have not hiked every canyon throughout this expansive region, my choices reflect over twenty years of extensive hiking coupled with comprehensive research in my own quest to explore the best of what the Colorado Plateau offers to those who seek its grandeurs.

In this chapter I will attempt to provide a full scope of information so you can fully enjoy each of these wonderful journeys. I describe each trail with enough practical detail as I believe necessary, but I avoid being overly detailed since I find it tends to cause more confusion. The trails included in this book can and will change over time. The administrative agency overseeing the area may move a trail if it is causing excessive wear to a sensitive area. Boulder and log jams are impermanent obstacles and may shift, forming new obstructions and changing the trail dramatically. Even trail signs can be different or non-existent as vandalism, weather, winds, and wear may occur. Anyone undertaking these excursions should possess a practical knowledge in the use of compass and map.

The sun setting in the Needles District, Canyonlands National Park

Please note that I did not include GPS coordinates; none of these hikes require a GPS to safely explore the area as long as you have a decent sense of direction. All mileages are approximate and are, for the most part, the accepted lengths and or hiking times issued by the administering authority for each hike, although my state-of-the-art GPS unit usually recorded hiking distances up to one-third longer than these accepted lengths.

The maps I have included in this book are for illustrative use only and are not recommended for use in land navigation. For each of these hikes (the only exception being Antelope Canyon, where paid guides accompany you), always have a good quality topographic map, a compass, and the practical knowledge to use them if necessary.

And now, without further adieu, here are what I consider the best canyon hikes in the American Southwest....

Antelope Canyon

Navajo Tribal Lands

Arizona

⚉ Claim to Fame:

Antelope Canyon is one of the world's most spectacular slot canyons, filled with magnificently sculpted orange-pink sandstone. It has also become the most-visited and most-photographed slot canyon in the American Southwest. Located near Page, Arizona, on Navajo Tribal Lands, this hike is actually made up of two distinct sections of canyon divided by State Route 98. Upper Antelope Canyon (south), also referred to as "The Crack," has more of an inverted V-shape, while Lower Antelope Canyon (north), also called "The Corkscrew," is more V-shaped, as this canyon drainage system flows north into Lake Powell.

In 1997 eleven people drowned exploring the canyon when they were caught in a flash flood, thrusting this beautiful little slot into the world spotlight and subsequently opening the proverbial door to masses of folks visiting the canyon on a daily basis. The hikes themselves are pretty easy strolls, staying within the confines of the canyon's walls, with the lower canyon providing a bit of simple climbing on steel ladders. Some folks will consider Antelope Canyon more of a photo-op than a hike, but visitors are required to perambulate, so I've included it in this book, and no one can deny the beauty of this gorgeous canyon. With all its popularity in recent years the sense of adventure and solace that previously existed is now completely gone, but once you've entered this surreal landscape you are sure to be unequivocally mesmerized by the sheer beauty of these slots!

⚉ Park Overview:
⚉**Closest town:** Page, AZ (4 miles)
⚉**Park elevations:** 4,000–4,120 feet
⚉**Park established:** 1964
⚉**Area:** 17 million acres (Navajo Nation)
⚉**Annual visitation:** Officially unknown, but reportedly "thousands each year" (although at times it can feel like thousands each day).

⚉ Getting There:
⚉**Airport:**
♦Page Municipal Airport, Page, AZ (4 miles)
♦Sky Harbor Airport, Phoenix, AZ (282 miles)
♦McCarran Airport, Las Vegas, NV (298 miles)

⚉**Vehicle:**
♦From US Highway 89 near Page, Arizona, take State Route 98 (just south of Page) and head west for 2 miles as you watch Navajo Generating Station getting closer. As you head down into a long dip in the road, look for Antelope Canyon Park at the bottom of the dip, at the

intersection with Antelope Point Road on the left (north). The park occupies both sides of the road. Upper Antelope will be on the right (south). For Lower Antelope, turn left (north) onto Antelope Canyon Road, then take the first left. On either side of the highway you'll see obvious parking areas and concession booths.

♦From State Route 98 eastbound, you'll find Antelope Canyon Park about 1 mile past the Navajo Generating Station, the area's most noticeable landmark. The park occupies both sides of the road: Upper Antelope will be on the left (south). For Lower Antelope turn right (north) onto Antelope Canyon Road, then take the first left. On either side of the highway, you'll see obvious parking areas and concession booths.

∾ Contact:
○**Web:** www.navajonationparks.org
○**Phone:** (928) 698-2808
○**Mail:** Lake Powell Navajo Tribal Office, P.O. Box 4803, Page, AZ 86040

∾ The Layout:
Antelope Canyon is one of the most accessible of the premier slot canyons in the Southwest and thus has become extremely touristed. The busiest time of year is between April and October. This is especially true inside Upper Antelope Canyon between about 11 a.m. and noon during the busy season, when narrow shafts of light can be pho-

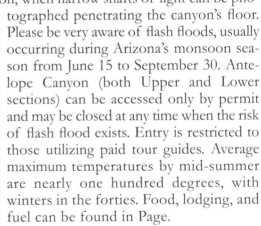

tographed penetrating the canyon's floor. Please be very aware of flash floods, usually occurring during Arizona's monsoon season from June 15 to September 30. Antelope Canyon (both Upper and Lower sections) can be accessed only by permit and may be closed at any time when the risk of flash flood exists. Entry is restricted to those utilizing paid tour guides. Average maximum temperatures by mid-summer are nearly one hundred degrees, with winters in the forties. Food, lodging, and fuel can be found in Page.

∾ Fees, permits, and restrictions: Open
seven days a week, 8 a.m. to 5 p.m. Call first during the winter season. The Navajo Nation recreational fee is $6 per person (small

Beautiful sculpted rock adorns Upper Antelope Canyon

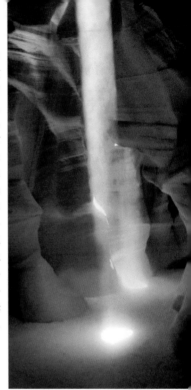

children free) and allows entry to both the Upper and Lower Antelope canyons, along with other tribal parks on that day. There is also a tour fee (usually $20–$25 per person, but up to $40 per person during prime time). As of May 2011, there is a one- to two-hour limit to the time you are allowed to spend in either upper or lower canyons, depending on the season. Separate fees are charged for the Upper and Lower canyon tours. Tour guides are usually on site, but in winter when visitation is low (or if you don't want to wait for a guide), consider calling ahead or booking a tour guide from the various guiding concessions listed on the Internet at www.NavajoNationParks.org. Dogs are not allowed inside these canyons, save for registered service dogs. This canyon is located on private property.

≋ Trail Overview:

This trail is a short day hike.

☼**Length:** Upper Antelope is 0.5 miles round-trip; Lower Antelope is one mile round-trip

☼**Difficulty:** Easy

☼**Elevations:** Upper Antelope: 4,140–4,210 feet; Lower Antelope: 3,996–4,094 feet

☼**Hiking times:** 2 hours maximum allowed in each section (only one hour during the busy season)

☼**Water availability:** No

☼**Toilets:** Toilets are located in the parking areas.

☼**Special advisories:** Summer can be extremely hot, with temperatures exceeding one hundred degrees. This is a dangerous slot canyon and prone to flash flooding, particularly during Arizona's monsoon season from mid-June through September. Always respect the guide's decision to close the canyon when he or she feels it is appropriate.

≋ Trailhead Directions:

For Upper Antelope Canyon, you will be required to pay the Navajo Nation recreational fee prior to entering the parking area. After parking your vehicle, check-in at the concession booth and pay the tour fee. You will be assigned a shuttle vehicle and guide who will take you to the canyon's entrance.

For Lower Antelope Canyon, enter the parking area just off Antelope Point Road and park your vehicle. Check in at the concession booth and pay the recreational fee and the tour fee. A guide will walk you to the canyon's entrance, which begins about one hundred feet from the concession booth.

≈ Trail Description:
☼ Upper Antelope Canyon — *The Crack*

Upper Antelope is the most visited and photographed of the two slots, but I find both Lower and Upper Antelope equally interesting. Part of the upper canyon's appeal is due to its unique photographic opportunities, as well as its relaxed, level walk along a sandy path (the lower canyon includes some ladder climbing and requires a bit of sure-footedness, and its tighter constraints can make it more difficult to capture photographically). This tour begins with a 2.5-mile 4WD shuttle to the nearly invisible opening into Upper Antelope Canyon.

As previously stated, the upper canyon is shaped more like an inverted V (like a tepee), is darker, and has a very different feel when compared to the lower canyon. The sandstone here appears to be a bit more buff color than in the lower canyon. The trail follows south for about a quarter-mile before suddenly opening into a wide dry wash. Some sections are wide and brightly lit while most segments are dark, making you feel like you've entered a cavern. From about mid-March through early October, around high noon, you may spot the often-photographed shafts of light penetrating the canyon. Take time to bask in the unique nature of this wonderful canyon as you turn and re-enter this narrow

Fantastic shapes abound inside Lower Antelope Canyon.

slot, returning the way you entered. Tour shuttles arrive at regular intervals to drive you back to the park's entrance by the highway.

✧Lower Antelope Canyon — *The Corkscrew*

From the concession booth you'll be guided to the entrance to the slot and briefed on the basic layout and rules. Your guide will usually accompany you through a portion of the canyon and then leave you on your own to explore.

The lower canyon heads north and begins as you shimmy into a tight crack in the earth just below a 60-foot-wide wash. Entering the cool depths, you'll drop down along steel ladders bolted into the canyon walls. This is a very different environment from the upper canyon. It is much more confined, with walls that narrow from more than twenty-five feet apart to only two feet. The walls have been sculpted over time into fantastic fins and swirls.

Early on, you'll probably recognize the famous "hole-in-the-rock formation" from canyon photographs, along with another favorite, "walk-through arch." Another series of ladders helps you descend the next drop-offs and continue on. You'll soon see a ladder that climbs out of the canyon, but it is an emergency escape route. After about a half-mile you'll reach the turn-around spot where you encounter an impassable 30-foot drop-off. You return, amazed and inspired, along the same route.

≈ Other Area Trails and Attractions:

✧**Buckskin Gulch:** The longest and one of the most beautiful slot canyons in the southwest. See details of this hike on page 20.

✧**Water Holes Canyon:** Another very nice slot canyon along US Highway 89 south of Page. A guide is required.

✧**Canyon X:** Canyon X is similar to Antelope Canyon and has become its alternative for photographers wanting shots of a pretty slot canyon without scads of people trampling through the scene. Canyon X also requires a paid guide.

✧**Glen Canyon National Recreation Area:** Comprised essentially of Lake Powell, this Colorado River reservoir and wonderland of water recreation contains nearly 2,000 miles of shoreline. Glen Canyon receives almost two million visitors annually, most of whom are there to enjoy the variety of water-related sports Lake Powell has to offer, but this NRA also has quite a few excellent hikes including Coyote Gulch (see page 32).

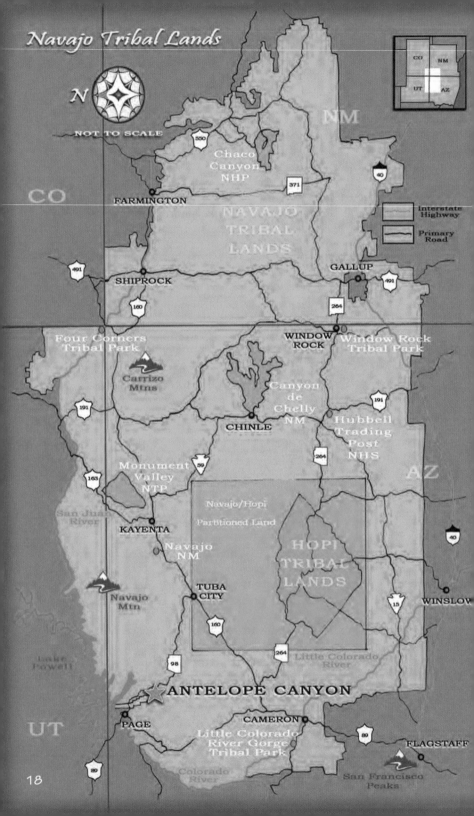

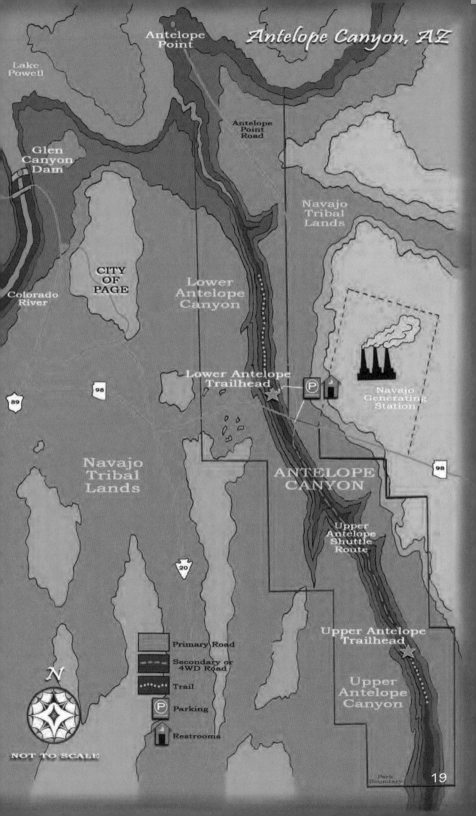

Antelope
Point

Antelope Canyon, AZ

Lake
Powell

Antelope
Point Road

Glen
Canyon
Dam

Navajo
Tribal
Lands

Colorado
River

CITY
OF
PAGE

Lower
Antelope
Canyon

Lower Antelope
Trailhead

Navajo
Generating
Station

98

89

Navajo
Tribal
Lands

ANTELOPE
CANYON

98

20

Upper
Antelope
Shuttle
Route

Upper Antelope
Trailhead

N

Primary Road

Secondary or
4WD Road

Trail

P Parking

Restrooms

Upper
Antelope
Canyon

NOT TO SCALE

Park
Boundary

19

Buckskin Gulch

Paria Canyon–
Vermilion Cliffs Wilderness
Utah

⩘ Claim to Fame:

Vermilion Cliffs National Monument is a treasure of absolutely striking geology, deep sinuous canyons, and towering scarlet cliffs. This sprawling park not only contains the colorful 3,000-foot escarpment known as the Vermilion Cliffs, but also the Paria Plateau, Paria Canyon, and Coyote Buttes. This hike actually takes place within the Paria Canyon–Vermilion Cliffs Wilderness, a region that nearly encircles and is essentially part of the national monument, and is administered by the Bureau of Land Management.

Buckskin Gulch is reportedly the longest slot canyon in the world, and it is considered the ultimate in slot canyons. This astounding gully snakes its way for nearly 18 miles to the Paria River, providing visitors with a subterranean voyage through layered sandstone as they travel downstream between its tight walls of etched and carved rock. Buckskin Gulch draws people the world over to its dramatic dark depths, letting hikers explore what is usually the domain of skilled canyoneers. Walls rise up to 500 feet in height, while narrowing down in some spots to less than 10 feet wide. With its west-to-east orientation, the sun will usually penetrate the canyon only around high noon, keeping this canyon fairly dark as the trail meanders on toward the Paria River Canyon. From the Buckskin Gulch and Paria Canyon confluence we'll head north along the Paria River and exit via White House Trailhead. This is a hike that will usually get you wet and muddy, but it's more than worth it to experience this extraordinarily awesome canyon—without a doubt one of the best slot canyons in the world.

⩘ National Monument Overview:
✧**Closest towns:** Page, AZ (32 miles), Kanab, UT (43 miles)
✧**Park elevations:** 3,100–6,500 feet
✧**Park established:** November 9, 2000
✧**Area:** 279,566 acres
✧**Annual visitation:** 47,000

⩘ Getting There:
✧**Airport:**
♦Page Municipal Airport, Page, AZ (35 miles)
♦Sky Harbor Airport, Phoenix, AZ (282 miles)
♦McCarran Airport, Las Vegas, NV (298 miles)

✧**Vehicle** (to BLM Paria Contact Station, open seasonally):
♦From Kanab, travel east on US Highway 89 for about 43 miles. There will be a BLM Contact Station sign on the right. Turn right (south) to the BLM Paria Contact Station, about 200 yards from the highway.

The author hiking inside spectacular Buckskin Gulch. (Photo by Nina Rehfeld)

♦From Page, travel west on US Highway 89 for about 32 miles. There will be a BLM Contact Station sign on the left. Turn left (south) to the BLM Paria Contact Station, about 200 yards from the highway.

⁑ Contact:
✿**Web:** www.blm.gov/az/vermilion/vermilion.htm
✿**Phone:** (435) 688-3200
✿**Mail:** Vermilion Cliffs NM, 345 E. Riverside Dr., St. George, UT 84790

⁑ The Layout:
Vermilion Cliffs National Monument and the Paria Canyon-Vermilion Cliffs Wilderness straddle the border of north-central Arizona and south-central Utah. Entry is gained via House Rock Valley Road, a gravel road accessed to the north from US Highway 89, and to the south from US Highway 89A (Alternate). Roads within the monument may be impassable when wet. There are no amenities inside the monument, but you can find lodging and services in Page, Arizona, and Kanab, Utah, or to the south at Jacob Lake, Arizona. This region is rough and remote, and like most areas on the Colorado Plateau, it is smokin' hot in the summer, with temps over 100 degrees in the shade. The biggest attractions at Vermilion Cliffs NM are Paria Canyon, Buckskin Gulch, and a photographer's dreamscape called The Wave.

The best time to hike Buckskin Gulch is late April through early June, and later on in October. (May permits go very fast so apply as early as possible.) This trail can be totally different depending on the season and current weather patterns. After wet periods the hike may require wading up to thigh deep in stagnant water known as the Cesspool, while mud can make progress slow as you try to gain traction. If you are lucky enough to go after a dry winter and spring there may be little to no water at all in the gulch until reaching Paria Canyon. Trying to hike this trail in cold winter months can be quite treacherous as the trail is often frozen over with ice, and hikers may repeatedly either slide on, or crash through, the ice into the freezing cold water below. In summer, not only is it incredibly hot, but on June 15 the Arizona monsoon season officially kicks off. Through the end of September, afternoon thunderstorms up to a hundred miles away can form suddenly, causing isolated, brief downpours and flash flooding in narrow canyons. Just what you don't want when you are inside a tight slot canyon with no escape! Again, if there is even a slight chance of rain, do not enter this or any slot canyon, ever.

〰 Permits and Restrictions:

Permits are required for both day hiking and overnight backpacking trips within Paria Canyon and Buckskin Gulch, and are available online by visiting their website. Fees are $6 per person, per day for day hiking, and $5 per person, per day for overnight trips. Dogs are allowed, but the fee applies to dogs too, so you'll have to pay to allow your pup to play.

〰 Trail Overview:

This trail description is from Wire Pass Trailhead through Buckskin Gulch and exiting at White House Trailhead, Paria Canyon. This route does require use of a shuttle vehicle. The trail can be done in sections as a day hike, an overnight trip, or a very long day hike.

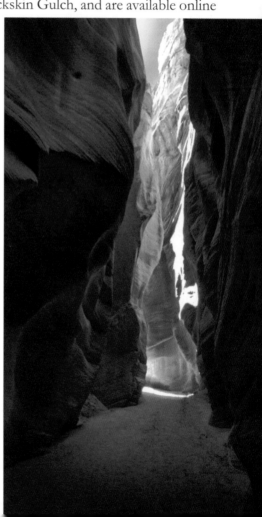

○**Length:** 21 miles
○**Difficulty:** Moderate (day hike) to strenuous (backpack)
○**Elevations:** 4,100–4,860 feet
○**Day-hike destinations:** Wire Pass Trailhead to Buckskin Gulch (one mile to first narrows), Buckskin Gulch Trailhead into the gulch (three miles to first narrows), or White House Trailhead

One of the first sections of narrows begins soon after entering Buckskin Gulch.

to Buckskin Gulch (3.5 miles to first narrows in Paria Canyon). Set your own turn-around time for each of these day hikes.

✪**Hiking times:** 10–12 hours

✪**Water availability:** Water in the gulch is usually muddy, murky, and stagnant, making it unsuitable for consumption, even with a filter. You are advised to carry all the water you'll need while hiking through Buckskin Gulch. If you are camping overnight at the confluence of Buckskin and Paria Canyons the springs and seeps near the junction have good water. In dry years, the only possible water source along this twenty-one mile hike may be at the confluence of Buckskin Gulch and Paria Canyon, although there are other springs beginning a few miles to the southeast inside Paria Canyon (water must be treated).

✪**Toilets:** Composting toilets are located at the trailheads.

✪**Special advisories:** Although no deaths have yet been recorded here, Buckskin Gulch is still considered one of the most dangerous hikes in the United States. This is due to its being a very tight and very long slot canyon where flash floods are a common occurrence. Always check the forecast before entering the gulch. The water can be extremely cold and the use of neoprene boots or socks is common for wading through this trail's numerous wet sections. If the Rabbit Hole is not open, about thirty feet of rope is required to lower packs down and provide a hand line at the boulder jam a mile-and-a-half from the Paria Canyon junction. There are no safe places to camp inside the gulch and no drinkable (or filterable) water until reaching Paria Canyon. The Middle Route, near the trail's midsection, is the one and only viable place to escape if need be. Hiking Buckskin Gulch should not be done solo unless you are a skilled canyoneer, as it often requires assistance from a hiking partner to transport packs over various boulder jams and other obstacles. All hikers must pack out their waste, so be prepared to pack out your poop. Quicksand is always a concern in Buckskin, but you'll never sink to your death. Injury usually occurs due to muscle strains from trying to pull your foot (or leg) out of the muck. Small rattlesnakes are also common within the confines of both Buckskin and Paria, so it pays to remain aware and focused during this trek.

≈ Directions to Wire Pass Trailhead:

♦From Kanab, travel east on US Highway 89 for about 39 miles, and turn right (south) to House Rock Valley Road. Proceed 8.3 miles to the Wire Pass parking area on the right (west).

♦From Page, travel west on US Highway 89 for about 34 miles, and turn left (south) to House Rock Valley Road. Proceed 8.3 miles to the Wire Pass parking area on the right (west).

༃ Directions to White House Trailhead:

◆From Kanab, travel east on US 89 for about 43 miles. There will be a BLM Contact Station sign on the right. Turn right (south) toward the Contact Station. Prior to reaching the BLM Paria Contact Station, you'll see a dirt road immediately to your left with a sign directing you to the White House Trailhead and campground. Follow this unimproved road for two miles to where it ends at the trailhead parking area and campground.

◆From Page, travel west on US Highway 89 for about 32 miles. There will be a BLM Contact Station sign on the left. Turn left (south) toward the Contact Station. Prior to reaching the BLM Paria Contact Station, you'll see a dirt road immediately to your left with a sign directing you to the White House Trailhead and campground. Follow this unimproved road for two miles to where it ends at the trailhead parking area and campground.

༃ Mileage between Trailheads: 15.5 miles

༃ Trail Description:

Note: While it is possible to begin your hike at the Buckskin Gulch Trailhead, starting your exploration of Buckskin Gulch at the more popular Wire Pass Trailhead cuts off over 4 miles of unremarkable hiking, and therefore gets you into the nicest slots much earlier.

Wire Pass Trailhead is located across the road from the parking area, where you'll find a trailhead register and self-pay station for day

🌀 Side Step: Hoodoos

Tall, thin spires of rock rising up from arid basins are called hoodoos, and they are another geologic formation familiar throughout the plateau and especially prominent at Bryce Canyon. Also called goblins, tent rocks, and fairy chimneys, these formations are typically made from sedimentary rock topped with a less easily eroded stone worn into a column of variable thickness but loosely described as a totem-pole shape. Hoodoos can range from five feet up to heights exceeding a ten-story building. Early plateau inhabitants, the Paiutes, believed the columns were formed from corrupt people frozen into stone by the legendary Coyote. Unfortunately, hoodoos don't last a very long time in geologic terms. They can lose about two to four feet every hundred years due to erosion, so see them while you can—they won't be around forever.

hikers. The well worn path proceeds east, and you quickly encounter a steel cattle gate. Once through this little maze, continue following broad Wire Pass Wash as it meanders through a small valley bounded by red rocks and infused with a variety of desert vegetation. After about a half-mile you'll pass a trail that climbs up on the right (south-southeast), signed "Coyote Buttes." Do not take this trail: it leads to Coyote Buttes and The Wave, not Buckskin Gulch. (Special permits are required for hiking in The Wave, and they are especially difficult to secure, with only ten percent of applicants receiving a permit in any given month.)

Instead, drop into the wash, and within one mile from the trailhead you'll reach the first of a few sections of narrow slots where the walls close to about three feet wide as they simultaneously begin to rise. Soon after entering this initial slot, you'll encounter the first of many boulder jams that might require assistance from a hiking companion to lower packs. After 1.7 miles the canyon abruptly broadens as you approach the confluence of Wire Pass and Buckskin Gulch. Just prior to departing Wire Pass, look to your right (south wall) to see a large alcove. Just

past it, some Native American pictographs can be seen low along the same wall.

At the junction, take a right (south-southeast) and follow the boulder-strewn wash as it wends downstream. Before you know it, the canyon closes in and you'll proceed along the bottom of the gulch for the next few miles. Depending on weather conditions, the trail throughout the gulch could be sandy and dry, or muddy and slick, and always rocky. About 7 miles from the trailhead, you will pass through an area of stagnant water called the Cesspool. At different times these nasty-smelling little lagoons can be waist deep, or completely dry. Soon after the Cesspool the canyon gets a bit deeper, darker, and more mysterious.

After 8 miles, the canyon's rim will begin to lower as you

The author reaches the confluence of Buckskin Gulch and Paria Canyon. (Photo by Larry Lindahl) approach the Middle Trail, which is not really a trail but more of an escape route or a side trail depending on your particular wants and needs at the time. The Middle Trail heads back up to the left (north) and is usually marked with a cairn. It's not too steep, but still a scramble to get up. Most people would not have a problem using this exit, but others may require a rope as a safety hand line, and to haul packs if need be. There are some not so easily spotted petroglyphs in the area, so take a little time to look around and explore before moving on.

Beyond the Middle Trail the canyon closes in again, becoming quite dark as you enter deeper, tighter slots once more. Nearly 12 miles into your hike (4 miles past the Middle Route), you'll encounter the most serious obstacle of the trip, the infamous mega-boulder-jam. This enormous yet short jumble of rocks can be circumvented at times by using the Rabbit Hole. This small opening under some of the rocks was blocked during a high water event some years ago but has reopened as of 2012, making it an easy traverse by dropping down into the hole then crawling through with no need to even remove your pack. If the Rabbit Hole is closed, the other option is to climb the rock jam to the left side and use the rope you brought to haul packs and help

The longest slot canyon in the world beckons with plenty of sculpted scenes like this.

lower yourself down along some rough-hewn foot holds in the rock wall. Often there are already ropes in place, but they cannot be relied upon to be in good working order, and they could be removed at any time. The obstacle is usually no problem; just take your time and you'll be through it before you know it.

A short distance below the boulder jam, you should notice the trail starting to get a little moist as a series of seeps running down the wall begins forming a small stream; these are usually a good place to obtain water if they have not dried up. The canyon walls soon rise to nearly 500 feet, and about 1.5 miles past the mega-boulder-jam (nearly 14 miles from the trailhead), you'll reach the confluence of Buckskin Gulch and Paria Canyon. A few nice camp sites are located just prior to the junction of the two canyons, but you may have to share a site during the busy season (May). These sites are your best bet if you are staying overnight because the next camps safe from flash flooding are located in Paria Canyon either a half-mile south (downstream) or at least a couple of miles upstream.

Pay attention: the confluence of Buckskin Gulch and Paria Canyon appears very similar to what you have been hiking through, and you could miss the left (north) turn if you are not cognizant of the opening. Continue heading north (upstream) along Paria Canyon for about a half-mile to Slide Rock Arch, which isn't really an arch but a massive slab of sandstone that broke loose from the east wall and crashed into the river. Paria Canyon is a bit wider than Buckskin here, but still visually and geologically interesting to hike through. From Slide Rock Arch the canyon meanders slowly north as the narrows begin to diminish. About 3.5 miles from Buckskin Gulch (17.5 miles total) the canyon walls open into a broad sandy wash. Hiking through this section you may spot (if you try really hard) more pictographs along the left (west) wall. After slogging through the sand another two miles, you will spot the Paria Windows—sections of low alcoves carved by water into the cliff wall on your right (east).

Just over a mile-and-a-quarter past the Paria Windows are the remains of the old White House Homestead (and trailhead namesake), which is located out of sight along the east side of the canyon. The cabin burned down during the 1890s, and there is only a loose stone foundation left here to view.

At 7.5 miles from Buckskin Gulch (nearly 21 miles from Wire Pass Trailhead), you should see a couple of narrow four-feet tall, brown trail markers on each side of the wash directing you to the White House Trailhead. Climb this sandy break in the river bank to access the trailhead and parking area, and congratulate yourself for having just completed one of the most gorgeous and arduous hikes the American Southwest has to offer.

⠿ Trail Options:
You could choose to day hike from Buckskin Gulch Trailhead into some nice narrow sections as it winds its way more than four miles to the Wire Pass Junction. Or alternatively, you can day hike from Wire Pass to the entrance of Buckskin. Cutting north-northwest toward the official Buckskin Gulch Trailhead will also take you to those same narrow sections.

Generally, folks day hike into Buckskin from Wire Pass and continue toward Paria Canyon for many miles through some of the nicest sections of Buckskin Gulch, until hitting their set turn-around time and heading back to Wire Pass. Many others day hike down from White House Trailhead and Campground in Paria Canyon, hiking a short distance up Buckskin before turning around and heading back. Backpackers can do the whole route from Buckskin Gulch into Paria Canyon and then hike along the Paria River all the way to its end, over forty-three miles away at Lees Ferry. Here again, a shuttle vehicle would be needed.

∼ Mileage Log from the Trailhead:
✧**Trail junction to Coyote Buttes and The Wave:** 0.5 miles
✧**First narrows in Wire Pass:** 1 mile
✧**Confluence of Wire Pass and Buckskin Gulch:** 1.7 miles
✧**The Cesspool:** 7 miles
✧**Middle Trail escape route:** 8 miles
✧**Boulder jam:** 12 miles
✧**Confluence of Buckskin Gulch and Paria Canyon:** 14 miles
✧**Slide Rock Arch:** 14.5 miles
✧**Narrows end:** 17.5 miles
✧**White House Trailhead:** 21 miles

∼ Other Area Trails and Attractions:

✧**The Wave:** Coyote Buttes is one of the most difficult places to get a permit even to day hike because of The Wave, an amazingly swirled and sculpted area where three drainages come together to form a sandstone junction of roiled wavy rock. The Wave is a photographer's paradise, but only ten percent of permit applications are granted for this extremely popular region.

✧**Antelope Canyon:** Another photographer's Mecca with two gorgeously sculpted slot canyons just a few miles west of Page, AZ. (See Antelope Canyon Trail on page 12 for more details.)

✧**Glen Canyon NRA:** Comprised essentially of Lake Powell, this Colorado River reservoir and wonderland of water recreation contains nearly 2,000 miles of shoreline. Glen Canyon receives almost two million visitors annually, most of which are there to enjoy the variety of water-related sports Lake Powell has to offer, but there are also quite a few excellent hikes within this national recreation area, including Coyote Gulch (see page 32).

Paria Canyon - Vermilion Cliffs Wilderness

98

N

NOT TO SCALE

Lake Powell

Antelope Canyon
Navajo Tribal Park

——— Primary Road

– – – Secondary or
4WD Road

········· Trail

PAGE

Glen Canyon
NRA

89

89

Grand
Staircase -
Escalante
NM

Lees Ferry

BIG
WATER

Grand
Staircase -
Escalante
NM
Visitor
Center

To
Flagsta

Colorado
River

89A

UT

PARIA CANYON-
VERMILION CLIFFS
WILDERNESS

White House
Campground

Vermilion
Cliffs
NM

Paria
River

Paria
Contact
Station

89

House
Rock
Valley
Road

BUCKSKIN GULCH

Stateline
Campground

CO

NM

UT

AZ

AZ

89A

67

To
Grand Canyon
North Rim

30

To
Kanab

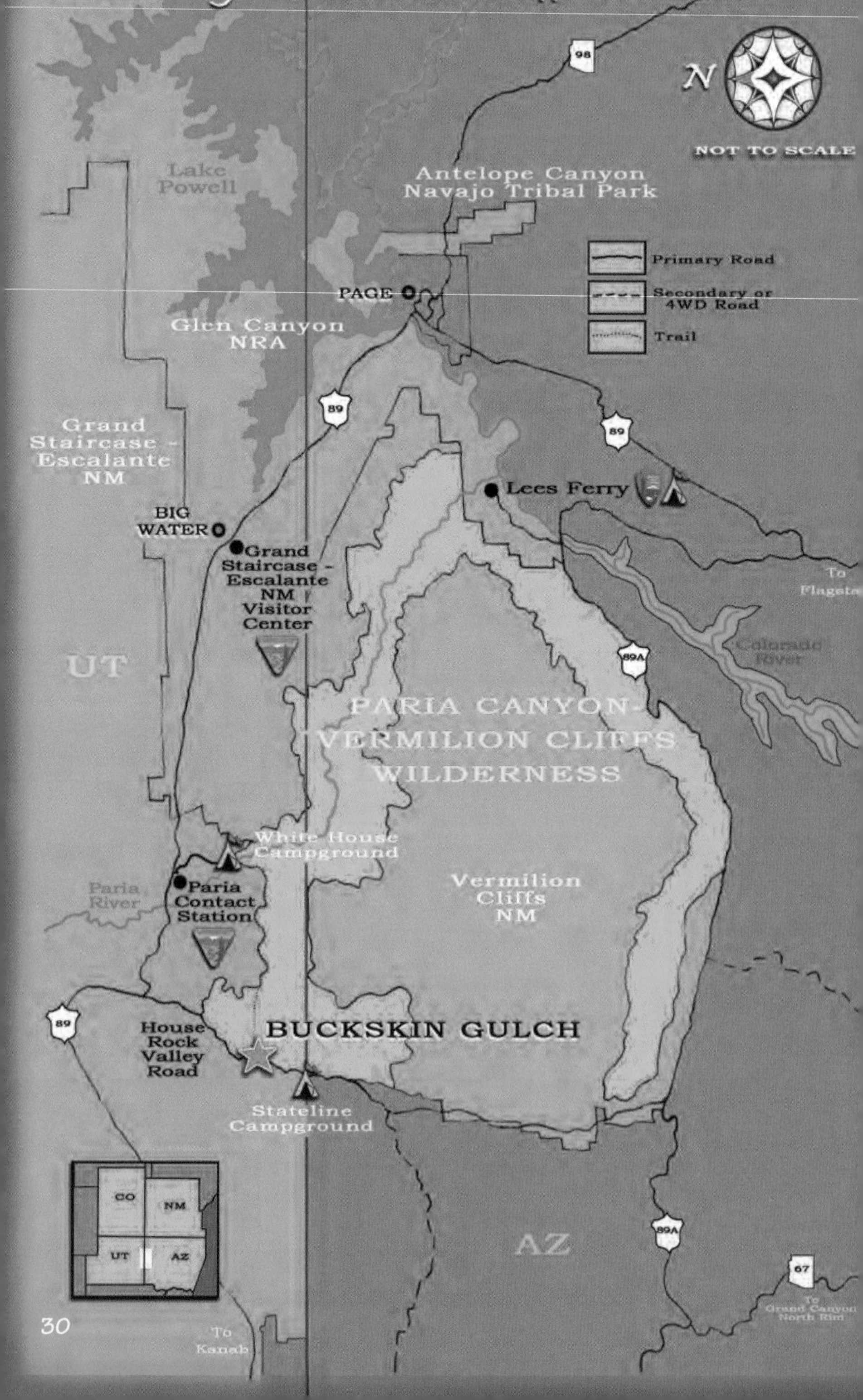

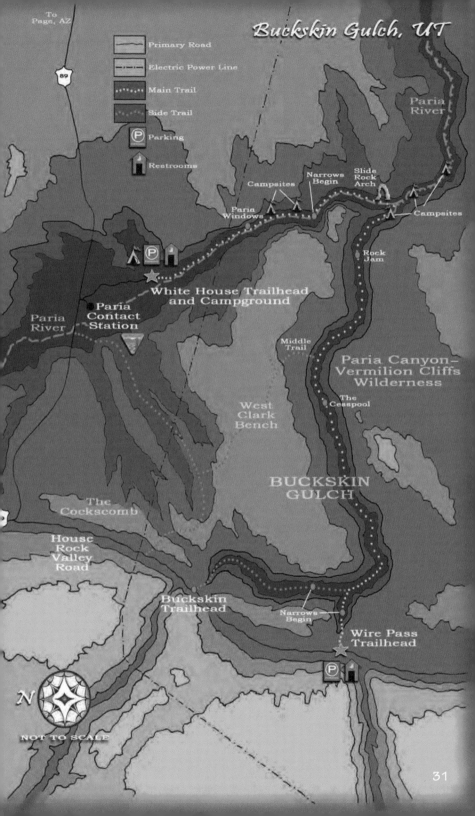

Coyote Gulch

Glen Canyon National Recreation Area & Grand Staircase–Escalante Nat'l Monument

Utah

⚹ Claim to Fame:

Grand Staircase–Escalante National Monument covers a huge swath of the Colorado Plateau. It contains 1.9 million acres of astoundingly beautiful and diverse terrain, including a variety of canyons, cliffs, and plateaus. Rugged and remote, it was the last place to be mapped in the lower United States and encompasses three distinct regions: the Grand Staircase, the Kaiparowits Plateau, and the Canyons of the Escalante. Covering a larger area than Rhode Island and Delaware combined, it is the largest tract included in the National Conservation Lands (an assortment of some 27 million acres that includes national monuments, conservation areas, wilderness areas, scenic rivers and historic trails, numbering some 866 units in the western states).

On the other hand, Glen Canyon National Recreation Area, while offering a few choice hikes, is best known for containing Lake Powell. Its dam-flooded canyons attract over a million tourists each year, who explore its waterways in houseboats, kayaks, jet skis, and powerboats. Encompassing more than 1.2 million acres, this "water park" was established in 1972 and contains more than 2,000 miles of shoreline. The lake began filling behind Glen Canyon Dam in 1963 and radically altered the naturally dry, multi-canyoned landscape by becoming the second largest reservoir in the United States. Lake Powell's Escalante Canyon tributary is one of the most gorgeous canyons along the Colorado Plateau.

Although remote, this hike may turn out to be one of the best you've ever done, its remoteness only adding to its allure. Coyote Gulch, a tributary of the Escalante River, has it all: sheer canyon walls, two arches, a natural bridge, shimmering creeks, waterfalls, and Native American pictographs. What more would you want? Well, perhaps a bit more solitude, but if you are hiking in spring or fall, you should expect to encounter other hikers along the way. So please be cognizant and respectful of others as you explore this gorgeous natural wonder.

⚹ Area Overview:
✪**Closest town:** Escalante, UT (39 miles)
✪**Park elevations:** 3,200–8,300 feet
✪**Park established:** October, 27, 1972 (Glen Canyon NRA),
September 18, 1996 (Grand Staircase–Escalante NM)
✪**Area:** 1.9 million acres (Grand Staircase–Escalante NM);
1.2 million acres (Glen Canyon NRA)
✪**Annual visitation:** 1,832,378 (Glen Canyon NRA)

⚹ Getting There:
✪**Airport:**
♦Grand Junction Regional Airport, Grand Junction, CO (280 miles)
♦Salt Lake City Airport, Salt Lake City, UT (290 miles)
♦McCarran Airport, Las Vegas, NV (300 miles)

☼Vehicle:

♦Grand Staircase–Escalante NM is bordered by two highways, US Highway 89, roughly between Panguitch, Utah, and Page, Arizona, and Utah State Route 12 from Panguitch to Boulder, Utah. For this trail, take SR 12 until you reach Hole-in-the-Rock Road (sometimes referred to as the Glen Canyon Recreational Area Road). The turnoff is about five miles southeast of Escalante, or twenty-two miles southwest of Boulder.

⁓ Contact:

☼**Web:** www.blm.gov/ut/st/en/fo/grand_staircase-escalante
☼**Phone:** (435) 644-4300
☼**Mail:** Grand Staircase–Escalante NM, Kanab Headquarters, 190 East Center, Kanab, UT 84741

⁓ The Layout:

The trail begins in Grand Staircase–Escalante National Monument, though the hike itself is largely within the Glen Canyon National Recreation Area. These public lands occupy such a large area of south-central Utah that combined they make up nearly 7 percent of the total size of the state. The trailhead is extremely remote, and most of the roads are dirt, gravel, or clay surfaced and can be impassable when wet. Make sure when you set out for the backcountry that you have a full tank of gas. High-clearance four-wheel drive vehicles are highly recommended. Hiking here is predominantly on undeveloped trails and proper route-finding skills are required. There are access roads into Grand Staircase–Escalante at multiple points around its circumference, but no amenities of any kind, except for three developed campgrounds. Glen Canyon NRA is almost exclusively accessed by various watercraft via the massive water body of Lake Powell. Treated water is generally

View from the back side of Jacob Hamblin Arch

Water flowing through Coyote Gulch creates numerous waterfalls and cascades.

not available within the monument's boundaries. Most people visit the Escalante region in spring and fall when temperatures are usually mild, while Lake Powell sees regular visitation through the summer months when water-related activities dominate. Most visitors to Coyote Gulch will backpack into the gulch on day one, day hike the remainder of the trail to Escalante Canyon and Steven's Arch on the second day, and pack out on the third day.

⌇ Permits and Restrictions:
Permits for all overnight stays in the backcountry are required. They are free, and they are available at the trailhead, or at the various visitor centers encircling the monument. The closest visitor center to the trailhead is the Escalante Interagency Visitor Center, 755 West Main Street, Escalante, UT. (435) 826-5499. Group size is limited to 12, campfires are not allowed, and pets are not allowed on the trail, so plan accordingly. Mountain bikes are allowed only on roads, and not allowed on the trails.

⌇ Trail Overview:
This trail is usually done as an overnight backpack trip from Hurricane Wash to Escalante River, or as a long day hike from Hurricane Wash to Jacob Hamblin Arch.
◌**Length:** 27 miles round-trip
◌**Difficulty:** Moderately strenuous
◌**Elevations:** 3,660–4,570 feet
◌**Day-hike destinations:** Jacob Hamblin Arch (14 miles round-trip)
◌**Hiking times:** 2–3 days
◌**Water availability:** Creek water is usually available in Coyote Gulch, but it must be treated. (There is generally no water for at least the first four miles along Hurricane Wash.)

✪**Toilets:** None at the trailhead, but two composting toilets are located inside Coyote Gulch.

✪**Special advisories:** You should already know that summer heat along the plateau can be brutal. Coyote Gulch is no exception, especially in the open wash. Always carry extra water supplies. Flash floods are a problem when hiking in any narrow slot canyons. Make sure you know the weather forecast before entering the canyon. Pets are prohibited from entering Coyote Gulch. Campfires are not allowed in the back-country, and human waste must be packed out using a sanitary bag system, unless you use one of the few backcountry toilets along this trail. During the cold season, neoprene socks can be very helpful to keep your feet warm while hiking through the cold waters of the gulch. Voices can echo long distances inside the canyon; please observe quiet hours after dark.

≈ Trailhead Directions:

Hurricane Wash is the easiest, most popular access into Coyote Gulch. To reach the trailhead, take State Route 12 until you reach Hole-in-the-Rock Road (sometimes referred to as the Glen Canyon Recreation Area Road). The turnoff is about five miles southeast of Escalante, or twenty-two miles south-southwest of Boulder. Most of the road runs south-southeast.

Hole-in-the-Rock Road is a wide, well-maintained yet rough, gravel and dirt road. You'll have Fortymile Mountain on your right as you drive 33.8 miles of this bone-rattling washerboard road to the Hurricane Wash Trailhead. The signed parking area is on the right (west) side of the road. The trailhead is across the road.

≈ Trail Description:

The trail begins across the road from the parking area. Follow the sandy wash as it heads east-northeast in the wash. The hiker registration box is located about a quarter-mile up the wash. The beginning of the trail is open range, and at about three-quarters of a mile you'll encounter the first of two cattle gates, allowing hikers through while restricting cattle. Most of the time Hurricane Wash Trail follows an old road, although it doesn't appear the road has been utilized by vehicles for many years. Slogging through the sandy wash can seem relentless, but it is a very pretty trail that just gets better and better. The trail splits in a few places, so make sure to confirm that you are following human foot-prints and not striding along a cow path. Continue hiking in the wash as the canyon walls slowly climb higher.

At three miles you will enter Glen Canyon National Recreation Area, marked by a large sign. Soon the canyon narrows to about twenty feet, then widens out again, and before you know it, you will pass around the second cattle gate. As you proceed you will begin to see more willows and cottonwood trees, and the walls climb up to 250 feet, as the canyon tightens. At this point, you may begin to see a bit of water in the creek, and at 5.5 miles (approximately two to three hours into the hike) you'll reach the intersection of Hurricane Wash and Coyote Gulch.

From here, head right (downstream) in a creek that has a bit more water volume. The trail stays mainly in the creek as it continues on its way to the Escalante River, occasionally crossing back along the overland sides of the streambed to cut corners. After hiking in and out of the stream and passing many sandy campsites, Jacob Hamblin Arch will come into view. The arch is named for a Mormon pioneer who served as a scout and missionary under Brigham Young. You'll have traveled just over seven miles from the trailhead to this point.

After passing a huge sheltered alcove and moving along the backside of Jacob Hamblin Arch, you'll see the first signed toilet on the right. The trail constricts tightly at 8.5 miles as the creek trickles down cascades of sandstone and the trail drops down to the creek again. At

John Ducasse pauses underneath Coyote Natural Bridge.
Since water has undercut its opening it is not considered an official arch, but a natural bridge.

Deeply carved rock inside Coyote Gulch

9 miles you pass underneath Coyote Natural Bridge (50-foot span) and not long after that, you will find yourself entering an open area with long, broad alcoves. Look for pictographs and remnants of early inhabitants off to the side of the alcoves.

Continue downstream as the trail goes in and out of the streambed, staying mostly in the creek. From here the going is relatively easy, save for a couple tricky spots. At 11 miles, Cliff Arch (also called Jug Handle Arch) is visible. When you encounter the first waterfall, you should pass along its right side. At the second waterfall below the arch, you'll need to follow along the ledge to the right (south wall), and after about a hundred feet you'll see the spot where you can slide back down. At the third waterfall, stay right, and you'll soon pass the second toilet on the left prior to reaching the fourth waterfall, where you should again stay to the right.

Thirteen miles from the trailhead is the last obstacle, a huge boulder jam at Crack-in-the-Wall junction. Bypass the rocks by following the trail on the right across a lower sand bank and then crossing up along a precipitous slickrock slope, staying low near the edge. This ledge will end above the creekbed where there is a double-stepped stump dug in next to the shelf to assist in the last descent. Meander a short ways downcanyon, until you reach the confluence of the Escalante River at about 13.5 miles from Hurricane Wash Trailhead.

For views of Stevens Arch walk five hundred yards upstream from the confluence. To get a closer look you'll need to go left (upstream or north) in the Escalante River to the mouth of Stevens Canyon, about 1.4 miles away.

After relaxing at the Escalante River and maybe heading over to view Stevens Arch, return via the same wonder-filled route.

≈ **Trail Options:**

Quite a few other trailheads lead into Coyote Gulch. Red Well Trailhead is located about thirty miles down Hole-in-the-Rock Road, entering Upper Coyote Gulch (north of Hurricane Wash), adding about a mile to the total hiking distance to the Escalante River and back. Another choice for more experienced hikers is to hike off-trail from Chimney Rock to Hurricane Wash.

Past Hurricane Wash at mile 36 on Hole-in-the-Rock Road, a signed turnoff indicates the Fortymile Ridge Trailhead. Taking that left will lead you to two other access points, Jacob Hamblin Arch Trailhead and Fortymile Ridge Trailhead. Each route has its own worth, but both require more canyoneering skills and some sturdy rope. Either of these two trails offers an alternate exit other than returning via the same Hurricane Wash route, but for a loop hike you'll probably need two vehicles, using one to shuttle between the trailheads.

≈ **Mileage Log from the Trailhead:**
✿**Hiker registration box:** 0.25 miles
✿**Enter Glen Canyon NRA:** 3 miles
✿**Coyote Gulch:** 5.5 miles
✿**Jacob Hamblin Arch:** 7 miles
✿**Coyote Natural Bridge:** 9 miles
✿**Escalante River:** 13.5 miles

≈ **Other Area Trails and Attractions:**

✿**Peekaboo, Spooky, and Brimstone Gulches** are located along Hole-in-the-Rock Road prior to reaching Hurricane Wash. To reach these great day hikes in tight slot canyons from SR 12, turn left toward the trailhead about 26 miles on an unsigned spur road.

✿**Lower and Upper Calf Creek Falls** are beautiful hikes to splendid little waterfalls. These trailheads are located at the Calf Creek Recreational Area 11 miles south of Boulder, or about 15 miles north of Escalante along SR 12.

✿**Bryce Canyon and Capitol Reef National Parks** are obvious choices for a variety of hiking opportunities, including the Navajo/Peekaboo/Queen's Garden route at Bryce Canyon discussed on page 94, and Upper Muley Twist Canyon at Capitol Reef, page 102.

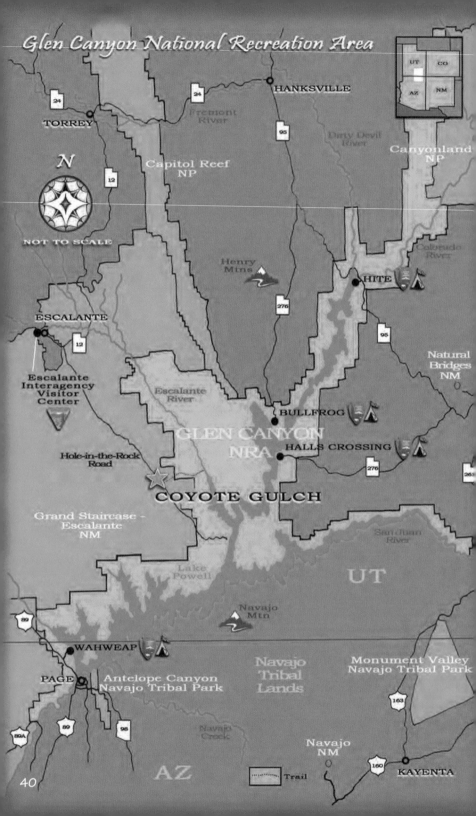

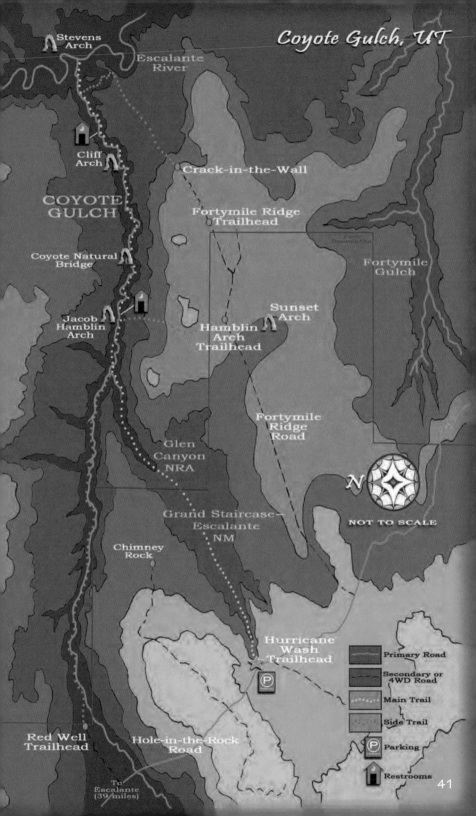

Devils Garden Primitive Loop
Arches National Park
Utah

≈ Claim to Fame:

This national park contains over 2,000 natural sandstone arches—the largest concentration in the world. While not the largest park, its unusual, numerous, and varied rock formations have created a fantastic landscape of colors and textures that draws over one million visitors each year. Here, the forces of erosion have exposed millions of years of geologic history, creating a surreal and beautiful landscape of exotic red rocks.

Devils Garden Trail is the longest maintained trail in the park at just over seven miles, including side trails and the Primitive Loop section. It is the second most popular trail in the park after Delicate Arch Trail, which means you won't get much solitude but you will explore seven arches (one of them spanning over 300 feet), visit the Dark Angel monolith, scramble on and around sandstone fins (at times between sheer vertical walls), and venture through the washes of Fin Canyon—all while basking in the beautiful and natural desert landscape. For the moderate exertion this trail requires, it is a journey no one should miss. It is simply a fun trail to hike.

≈ Park Overview:
✿**Closest town:** Moab, UT (5 miles)
✿**Park elevations:** 4,085–5,653 feet
✿**Park established:** April 12, 1929 (National Monument), November 12, 1971 (National Park)
✿**Area:** 76,519 acres
✿**Annual visitation:** 1,014,403

≈ Getting There:
✿**Airport:**
♦Grand Junction Regional Airport, Grand Junction, CO (110 miles)
♦Salt Lake City Airport, Salt Lake City, UT (230 miles)

✿Vehicle:
♦From I-70 in Utah, take Exit 180 (Crescent Junction/Moab) to State Route 191 and drive south for 25 miles to park entrance on left.

♦From the town of Moab, follow State Route 191 north 5 miles to the park entrance on right.

≈ Contact:
✿**Web:** www.nps.gov/arch
✿**Phone:** (435) 719-2299
✿**Mail:** Arches National Park, PO Box 907, Moab, UT 84532

⁓ The Layout:

Arches National Park is relatively small, encompassing just 120 square miles. Summers can be extremely hot (over 100 degrees). Winters are quiet and cold; spring through fall are, on average, the most temperate and experience high volumes of visitation. It is an easy park to navigate since there is only one main road, about twenty miles long. From the main road there are three spur roads, two paved and very touristed, and one lightly used unimproved road. Food, fuel, and lodging are not available inside the park but are found five miles south in the town of Moab.

⁓ Permits and Restrictions:

Open year round, 24 hours a day, $10 fee per vehicle or $5 per individual (motorcycle, bicycle, walk-in). Backpacking permits are required; obtain a free backcountry pass at the visitor center. Hikes in Fiery Furnace require a permit (fee charged).

⁓ Trail Overview:

This trail is a day hike.
⟡**Length:** 7.2 miles round trip, including spur trails and primitive loop
⟡**Difficulty:** Moderate, with some minor scrambling
⟡**Elevations:** 5,100–5,500 feet

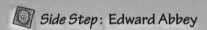

◉ *Side Step*: Edward Abbey

If I were to choose one iconic character who became known as the voice of the modern desert Southwest it would have to be Edward Abbey. Abbey found his utopia in the desert and used his extraordinary sense of word and prose to pen twenty-one books, nearly all of which dealt with his love of wilderness. His bibliography includes *The Brave Cowboy* (1956), *The Monkey Wrench Gang* (1975), and my personal favorite, *Desert Solitaire* (1968), in which he writes of his time spent as a park ranger at Arches National Monument and rails about his disgust for contemporary culture and unadulterated development, while including other lively vignettes concerning local society and the beauty of the natural world. A passionate and eloquent advocate for the preservation of the American Southwest, Abbey was an inspiration to many involved in environmental activism during the late 1960s. Pulitzer Prize-winning writer Edwin Way Teale said that Abbey was "a voice crying in the wilderness, for the wilderness." Lonesome Dove author Larry McMurtry, writing for the *Washington Post*, touted Abbey as "the Thoreau of the American West." It is a comparison that has stuck, although I can surmise that a nonconformist like Edward Abbey probably hated it.

○**Day-hike destinations:** Landscape Arch (2 miles round-trip), Double O Arch (5 miles round-trip)

○**Hiking times:** 4–5 hours, including spur trails and primitive loop

○**Water availability:** Drinking water is available seasonally at the trailhead.

○**Toilets:** Composting toilets are located at the trailhead.

○**Special advisory:** The park service discourages hiking this trail when the rock is wet or snowy. The trail is exposed and quite hot in summer; bring adequate water. Some exposures to height can require extra caution. The trail is well-signed until reaching the Primitive Loop, but hikers still need to remain attentive to trail clues along this route. Follow cairns closely, especially when hiking in canyon washes, as it is difficult to anticipate when the trail will exit the wash. Dogs are not allowed on trails within the park.

≈ Trailhead Directions:

Arches National Park is located along State Route 191, 5 miles north of Moab, Utah. Once inside the park, travel 19 miles to the end of the main road. The road terminates at the Devils Garden parking area, where there are only about 150 parking spaces that can quickly fill up. During the busy spring and fall hiking seasons your best bet is to arrive before 9 a.m.

≈ Trail Description:

The trailhead begins in the northwest corner of the parking lot where there is a large trail sign. The trail starts off on a groomed gravel surface and you quickly find yourself traveling between tall vertical walls and impressive finned formations as the path proceeds in a northwest direction. Less than a quarter-mile from the trailhead you will see the first spur trail on your right. Take this spur; the trail slopes down and almost immediately divides. If you turn right you will head south to Tunnel Arch (best seen in morning light). Look up to the west to see its round, tunnel-like window. If you turn left (north), you will reach the much more intriguing Pine Tree Arch. Which to visit first is your choice, and after viewing each arch you can return to the main trail.

At a little over three-quarters of a mile from the trailhead, you'll see a junction on the right where the Primitive Trail rejoins the main pathway. Most people stay to the left on the improved path and continue on as the trail turns sandy. You will soon reach spectacular Landscape Arch, still less than a mile from the trailhead. At nearly 300 feet

long, this delicate ribbon of rock is considered the longest natural rock span in the world. Gravity is constantly weighing on this massive rock expanse and someday a multitude of hiking and guide books will have to be rewritten when it eventually and inevitably falls. As a matter of fact, visitors used to be able to walk underneath the arch, but since the early 1990s pieces of rock have fallen from the arch, forcing the area to be fenced off.

Many visitors simply turn around at this point and head back to the parking lot, but this is where the trail starts getting interesting (and a bit more peaceful too). Continuing toward the northwest, the gravel path ends and becomes a rough trail climbing up on slickrock. You'll need to pay close attention to trail cairns (rock stacks) and signs, although the trail is easily followed if you pay proper attention. You'll soon encounter the effects of gravity firsthand as you trek

View from the trail to Private Arch

near the crumbled remains of what was once Wall Arch, now cordoned off. Wall Arch was the park's twelfth largest before it collapsed during the night of August 4, 2008. At about 1.4 miles you'll spot the next side trail on the left. This spur (slightly more than half-mile) takes you to Partition Arch, a double arch with a small side window, and Navajo Arch, a deeper alcove arch with plenty of shade. The spur trail crosses a sandy area and quickly reaches a fork. To the left is Partition Arch, while heading right will take you to Navajo Arch. Both are well worth the time. Both trails head southeast to the arches. After spending time with each, return again to the main trail, and its junction with the Partition/Navajo spur.

So far, you've hiked about 2.1 miles to reach this junction. Continue on the main trail following the familiar northwest tack. The trail moves through undulating sections of narrow slickrock fins and sandy washes, climbing up for expansive views across Salt Valley to the west and overlooking Fin Canyon to the east. At 2.3 miles you double back from the top of a long sandstone fin and drop into the wash using a well-placed log, soon reaching the next junction. The right (north) fork ends quickly at a viewpoint overlooking Black Arch, a dark shadow in the distance amongst the rolling fins to the east. The left (west) fork continues on toward Double-O Arch. This is the highest point of the trail, and the various fins you'll see were formed as the earth was forced upward, fracturing the upper layers of sandstone into these long, parallel ridges.

After a few minutes of hiking between fins and over slickrock, Double-O Arch will come into view. Still moving northwest, you will descend a fin as the convoluted trail curves left (west) amongst pinyon pines until you arrive at the foot of the huge opening called Double-O

Landscape Arch, measuring just over 290 feet in length, is considered the longest natural arch in the world.

Arch. This magnificent arch is one of the highlights of this excursion. To gain the best vantage point, you'll need to scramble up onto the lower arch, and then head left, ascending further as the sandstone curves around to the right.

Return to the main trail and bear left about forty feet from the arch, and you will soon encounter the triple trail junction. Heading left (northwest) takes you on a one-mile round-trip jaunt out to Dark Angel, a 150-foot monolith (the last remains of an ancient fin), and the northernmost section of the trail. Going right (northeast) takes you to the Primitive Loop section of the trail. After viewing Dark Angel, remember to turn left (northeast) when getting back on the main trail.

Once you start on the Primitive Trail, you'll see a park service sign with the dire warning "Caution, Primitive Trail, Difficult Hiking." While the remaining hike is similar to what you've already done, this sign is a reminder that if you are a novice hiker, with little route-finding experience, you may consider going back to the trailhead the same way you came. That said, if the area is not snowy or iced over, you should be fine as long as you pay attention to abrupt changes in direction, cairns and other trail signage.

The Primitive Trail drops down into a dry wash between rock fins and reaches the next signed junction at 4.5 miles. Taking a right (southeast) onto the spur trail at this junction will take you through a slot out to Private Arch (less than a half-mile round-trip). Return the way you came and head right (northeast) to continue on the Primitive Loop.

The trail descends along slickrock ledges and ramps. A couple of these ledges can feel a bit precarious, so be careful. The trail slowly curves to the southeast and down to the sandy wash of Fin Canyon. Once in the wash you'll head northeast for less than a quarter-mile, where you'll see a sign announcing the trail's departure from the wash. From that sign you should be able to see the next sign indicating "Main Trail" with an arrow pointing to the right. After climbing out from the canyon wash, the trail begins to level out a bit, heading predominantly south, becoming a well-defined sandy trail. The fins behind you fade from view as the desert opens up to sloped blackbrush range and the trail moves south to southeast, then back to the south again through some steeper sandy sections, making you work a little harder before leveling

Rock fins along the Primitive Loop

and reaching the familiar junction of the main trail and the Primitive Loop at 6.75 total miles. Go left (south) and retrace your route back to the trailhead.

⚭ Trail Options:
Most options have been mentioned in the trail description, including the two main turn-around points along the trail. The first is at Landscape Arch, where the developed trail ends (for a round trip just under two miles); the second is after visiting Double-O Arch (for a round trip just over 4.5 miles from the trailhead), a popular turnaround in lieu of traveling the whole Primitive Loop section. Another option is to hike the Primitive Loop first. You would get the least exciting sections over with, saving the better sights for last.

⚭ Mileage Log from the Trailhead:
✪**Pine Tree/Tunnel Arch fork:** 0.25 miles
✪**Primitive Trail junction:** 0.75 miles
✪**Landscape Arch:** 0.9 miles
✪**Partition/Navajo Arch junction:** 1.4 miles
✪**Double-O Arch/Black Arch Overlook junction:** 2.3 miles
✪**Double-O Arch:** 2.5
✪**Dark Angel monolith:** 3 miles
✪**Private Arch:** 4.5 miles
✪**Primitive/Main Trail junction:** 6.75 miles
✪**Return to trailhead:** 7.5 miles

⚭ Other Area Trails and Attractions:

✪**Delicate Arch Trail:** The trail to this stately arch is the most popular trail in the park, and takes hikers to a natural ringed amphitheater with an up-close view of this Utah icon.

✪**Tower Arch Trail:** This trail, located in Klondike Bluffs, the park's least utilized area out on Salt Valley Road, is another delightful trail.

✪**Canyonlands National Park:** Many beautiful hikes lie within the park's four distinct areas, The Needles, Island in the Sky, The Maze, and the rivers district. An especially splendid hike, Druid Arch Trail, is described on page 52.

✪**Deadhorse Point State Park:** Hikes lead to an iconic vista near Island in the Sky.

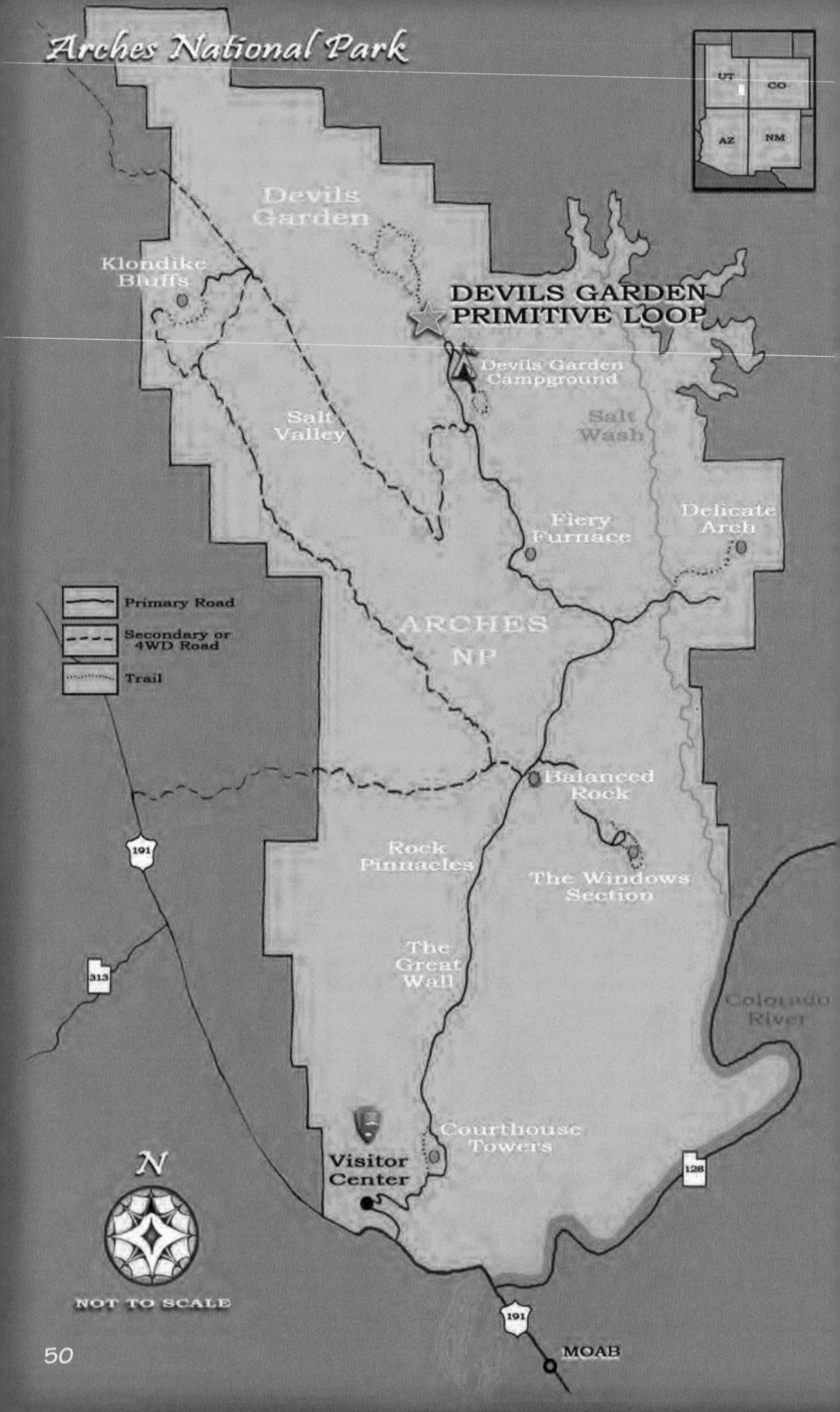

Arches National Park

UT
CO
AZ
NM

Devils Garden

Klondike Bluffs

DEVILS GARDEN PRIMITIVE LOOP

Devils Garden Campground

Salt Valley

Salt Wash

Fiery Furnace

Delicate Arch

ARCHES NP

Primary Road

Secondary or 4WD Road

Trail

Balanced Rock

Rock Pinnacles

The Windows Section

The Great Wall

Colorado River

191

313

Courthouse Towers

Visitor Center

N

NOT TO SCALE

128

191

MOAB

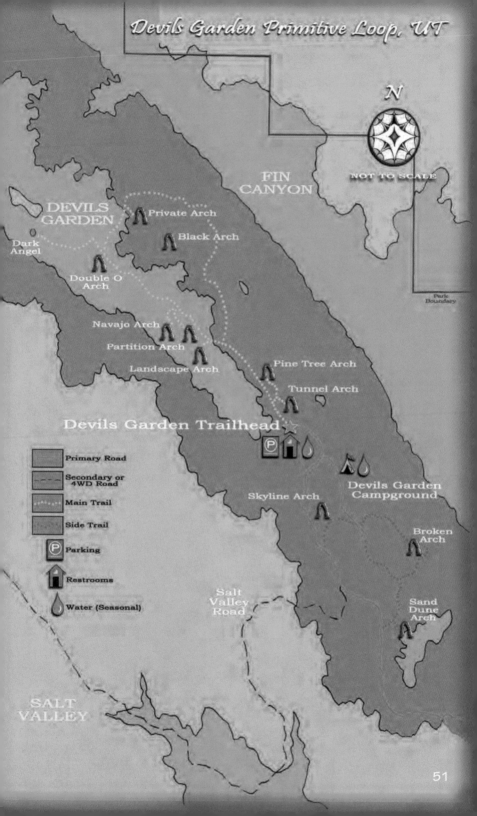

Devils Garden Primitive Loop, UT

FIN CANYON

N

NOT TO SCALE

Park Boundary

DEVILS GARDEN

Dark Angel

Private Arch

Black Arch

Double O Arch

Navajo Arch

Partition Arch

Landscape Arch

Pine Tree Arch

Tunnel Arch

Devils Garden Trailhead

P

Skyline Arch

Devils Garden Campground

Broken Arch

Sand Dune Arch

Salt Valley Road

SALT VALLEY

Legend

	Primary Road
	Secondary or 4WD Road
	Main Trail
	Side Trail
P	Parking
	Restrooms
	Water (Seasonal)

Druid Arch

Canyonlands National Park

Utah

≈ Claim to Fame:

Gorgeous multicolored canyons eroded into a multitude of stone shapes are the essence of Canyonlands National Park. Author Edward Abbey described this area as "the most weird, wonderful, magical place on earth—there is nothing else like it anywhere." Due to its isolation and primitive setting, this park receives fewer visitors, making it even more appealing to the more serious adventure-seeking outdoor folks.

This wonderful trail from Elephant Hill to Druid Arch offers some of the most spectacular views within the Needles district, if not the whole of this national park. Because the stately profile of Druid Arch rising up from its surrounding stone escarpment reminds many of Stonehenge, it was named for those who built that famous ancient rock structure in Wiltshire, England. Druid Arch began eons ago as a massive rock. The center caved in, and the remaining crumbled rock eroded away, leaving this magnificent natural structure. This trail is a visual treat of colorful spires, sandy washes, and sandstone benches, all beckoning hikers to come and explore.

≈ Park Overview:

✿**Closest towns:** Blanding, UT (70 miles), Moab, UT (75 miles)
✿**Park elevations:** 3,700–7,200 feet
✿**Park established:** September 12, 1964
✿**Area:** 337,598 acres
✿**Annual visitation:** 435,908

≈ Getting There:

✿**Airports:**
♦Grand Junction Regional Airport, Grand Junction, CO (150 miles)
♦Salt Lake City Airport, Salt Lake City, UT (270 miles)

✿**Vehicle:**
♦From Blanding, Utah, take State Route 191, heading north about 35 miles to SR 211 (left). Head west on SR 211 another 35 miles to the Needles Visitor Center.

♦From Moab, Utah, head south on State Route 191 40 miles to SR 211, turn right (west), and proceed on SR 211, 35 miles to the Needles Visitor Center.

≈ Contact:

✿**Web:** www.nps.gov/cany
✿**Phone:** (435) 719-2313
✿**Mail:** Canyonlands NP, 2282 SW Resource Blvd., Moab, UT 84532

Mushroom shaped rocks with the La Sal Mountains in the background

≋ The Layout:

Canyonlands National Park contains four distinct districts: the Needles, Island in the Sky, the Maze, and the rivers contained therein (Colorado and Green). The environment is high and dry desert with summer heat often exceeding 100 degrees and winter lows in the 20s. Most hiking activities take place in spring and fall. It is another area easily navigated because there is a single main road entering the Needles District with only a few short secondary roads leading to more than 60 miles of trail. There are campground facilities, but no food or lodging within the park. The closest amenities are located in Monticello, Blanding, or Moab, Utah.

≋ Permits and Restrictions:

Open year round, 24 hours a day, $10 fee per vehicle or $5 per individual (motorcycle, bicycle, walk-in). To overnight in the backcountry, a $15 permit is required and reservations (highly recommended) can be applied for no earlier than the second Monday in July for the next calendar year.

≋ Trail Overview:

Trail description is from the Chesler Park Trailhead. This trail can be done as a day hike or overnight backpack.

○**Length:** 11 miles
○**Difficulty:** Moderate to strenuous
○**Elevations:** 5,120–5,765 feet
○**Hiking times:** 5–6 hours
○**Water availability:** Seasonal water is available at Squaw Flat Campground.
○**Toilets:** Composting toilet at the trailhead.
○**Special advisories:** Trail is exposed and quite hot in summer; bring adequate water. Some exposures to heights can require extra caution. It is imperative that you follow cairns closely on this trail, especially when hiking in canyon washes, as you can never seem to anticipate when the trail will exit the wash. Always bring a map with you, or the multiple trails in this area could get all the more confusing.

⌇ Trailhead Directions:

From SR 191, head west on SR 211 (NOT the junction just north of the park entrance with a sign saying "Needles Overlook"). SR 211 is almost directly across from Church Rock (looks like a bell to me) along SR 191. Once on SR 211 drive 34 miles and you'll pass the Visitor Center on the right. Continue another 2.5 miles and follow the signs to Squaw Flat Campground. Take the right toward Campground Loop B. (Going straight would bring you to Campground Loop A.) The road to Loop B heads left, but you'll want to bear slightly to the right as the pavement ends and follow the sign to Elephant Hill. This road is unimproved but easily driven in a passenger car, ending in three miles at the parking area for Chesler Park Trail. The road essentially ends here, but if you have a high-clearance four-wheel drive vehicle it is possible to continue further to Devils Kitchen Camp and the Chesler Park Loop Trail.

⌇ Trail Description:

A few trails will get you out to Druid Arch, but the Elephant Hill Trailhead is the most popular, most accessible, and shortest route. You'll be starting out on the Chesler Park Trail, which begins on the southwest side of the parking area (The 4WD road will be on your right or northwest.) The trail heads in a southerly direction while climbing up through a narrow cleft on sandstone slab stairs until leveling out on a high slickrock bench, where you'll find a splendid open view.

After about a mile the trail passes through one of the wider openings in a row of jointed fins and slowly descends before leveling and continuing south-southeast. At 1.5 miles, you'll reach the first of many well-marked junctions. At this first junction, head right (west-southwest)

Druid Arch (a view from the back side)

toward Chesler Park. (Left or east would take you to Squaw Flat Campground.) The trail climbs on top of slickrock between fins and slips through another short rock joint opening into a large blackbrush basin. You'll be traveling along a divide with Big Spring Canyon to the east and Elephant Canyon due west, and soon you'll find yourself descending through a three-foot-wide, black-walled slot, and subsequently dropping down along steep rocky switchbacks into Elephant Canyon. At 2.1 miles from the trailhead, you'll reach the second junction.

Take a left (south) and continue on. (Going right leads to campsite EC1 and straight or west leads into the Needles, including Chesler Park and Devils Kitchen.) After turning left, proceed up the wash of Elephant Canyon about 40 feet, where the trail climbs up on the right. From here, the trail alternates between the wash and paralleling its banks. Before long, you'll see a conspicuous canyon that branches off toward the southeast, and when you get there you'll find the third junction at 2.9 miles. Proceed right (south-southeast). (Left would take you to Big Spring Canyon.) The trail is similar to the last section, alternating between walking in the wash and on its banks, and you'll pass a couple of campsites along the way until you reach the fourth junction at 3.4 miles.

Go left (south-southeast); otherwise you'll be heading toward Chesler Park and the Joint Trail. The trail changes back to slickrock as the canyon gets increasingly narrower. Around 3.7 miles from the trailhead, where two washes converge, bear left into the larger one, following a large cairn and moving toward the high canyon walls. At about 4.6 miles, turn left, following the cairns out of the wash. When I last hiked this area there was no sign indicating the trail. A good portion of the remainder of this hike is along the bench above the wash where

you will eventually see the arch, although it is barely recognizable from the side. The route basically ends when you encounter a steel ladder —after that it climbs a steep, rocky gully, leveling off near the end of Elephant Canyon at Druid Arch. Bask in the joy of hiking a beautiful trail and visiting this immense rock formation as you return along the same route.

≈ Trail Options:

If you want to vary your hike, and if you have the stamina and the navigational skills, head back via a different route. After leaving Druid Arch, you can take a left (west) toward Chesler Park. At the next two junctions turn right (the first takes you north, and the next heads east), and you will return to the second junction you en-

Some of the most wonderful rock formations in canyon country can be found within Canyonlands National Park.

countered in Elephant Canyon. From here, go back the same way you started. Another pleasant option is to backpack to any of the campsites along this trail or others in the vicinity and stay overnight inside one of the canyons. Permits are necessary for overnights in the backcountry; they are available at the visitor center or can be reserved in advance (postmarked or faxed). A $15 fee is required.

Otherwise, you can start the hike to Druid Arch from Squaw Flat Loop "A" Trailhead and down Big Springs Canyon, or if you have a high-clearance, four-wheel drive vehicle and the proper experience, you can drive the rough extension road out to the west side of Chesler Park and Devils Kitchen Campground (mentioned in the directions to the trailhead).

∼ Mileage Log from the Trailhead:
✿**First junction:** 1.5 miles
✿**Elephant Canyon (second junction):** 2.1 miles
✿**Third junction:** 2.9 miles
✿**Forth junction:** 3.4 miles
✿**Druid Arch:** 5.5 miles

∼ Other Area Trails and Attractions:

✿**Peekaboo Trail:** This trail passes Squaw and Lost Canyons before heading into Salt Creek Canyon. This hike takes you along high slickrock cliffs with magnificent views.

✿**Island in the Sky and Dead Horse Point State Park:** This northernmost region of Canyonlands National Park includes a few nice hiking trails and a wonderful drive with numerous overlooks.

✿**The Maze:** The Maze District is the least-visited area of Canyonlands National Park, as you must enter this remote region from the western side of the Colorado River. The nearest highway is SR 95 (at least a hundred miles away), and the roads are all 4WD, rough, and untamed, with absolutely no amenities. If you choose to enter this area you should be highly experienced in multi-canyon route finding over varied terrain, self-secure and self-sufficient. The payoff is getting to explore some geologically and naturally wild canyons in some of the most remote settings in the lower United States.

✿**Arches National Park:** Great hikes include Delicate Arch Trail and Devils Garden Primitive Loop described on page 42.

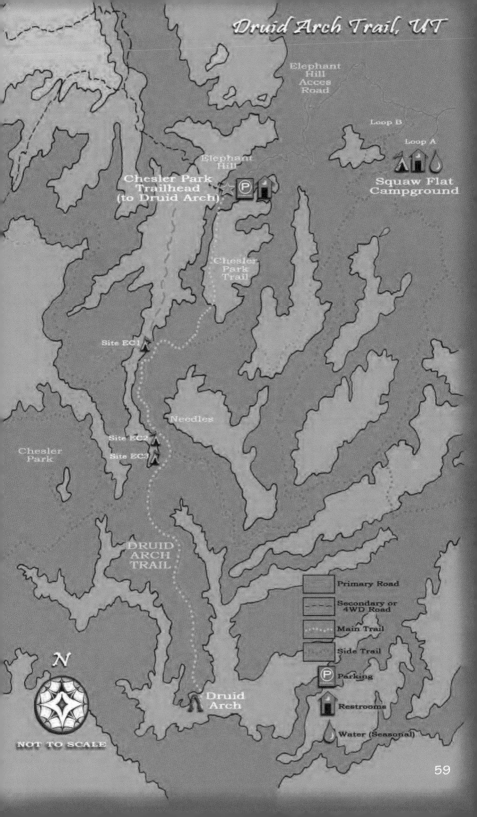

Druid Arch Trail, UT

Elephant Hill Acces Road

Loop B

Loop A

Squaw Flat Campground

Elephant Hill

Chesler Park Trailhead (to Druid Arch)

Chesler Park Trail

Site EC1

Needles

Site EC2

Chesler Park

Site EC3

DRUID ARCH TRAIL

Primary Road

Secondary or 4WD Road

Main Trail

Side Trail

Parking

Restrooms

Druid Arch

Water (Seasonal)

N

NOT TO SCALE

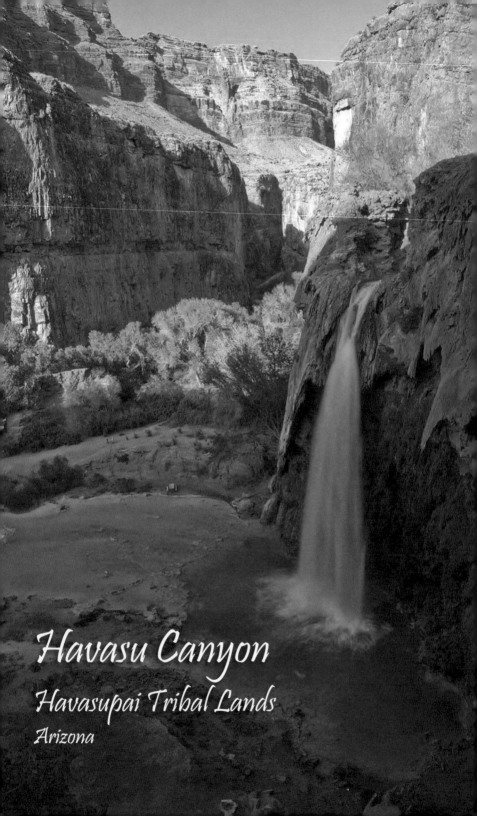

Havasu Canyon

Havasupai Tribal Lands

Arizona

⌇ Claim to Fame:

In Havasu Canyon, it is all about the water. This land of mystical blue-green waters contains some of the most spectacular waterfalls in the Southwest. Listed by many as one of the top ten journeys in the world, the canyon is often discussed in terms usually reserved for mythical places such as Shangri-la, Utopia, and the Garden of Eden. The canyon was changed dramatically in 2008 when a flash flood struck just south of the canyon, subsequently flooding areas of Supai Village and Havasu Campground, although the beauty of this wonderful region endures. The biggest alterations to the canyon from the flood concern the look and flow of water over the renowned Havasu Falls and the redirection of Navajo Falls into what is now being referred to as "New Navajo Falls."

The waterfalls of Havasu Canyon will always be changing in appearance, and Havasu Creek's resplendent turquoise stream shimmering within it will continue to beg visitors to play and explore. Havasu Canyon is the consummate destination for hikers of all levels. After a quick series of switchbacks, the hike down to the village and campgrounds is an easy but lengthy stroll, staying mostly in the winding wash of Hualapai Canyon, then moving easily into the forested trail of Havasu Canyon prior to reaching the village of Supai. The varied and plentiful waterfalls and cascades begin just beyond the town. The canyons themselves offer a delightful jaunt through a couple of chasms of varied natural charm, while the exquisite waterfalls will amaze and inspire all who venture into this paradise of red rock and crystalline blue-green waters.

⌇ Area Overview:

✿**Closest towns:** Seligman, AZ (95 miles), Peach Springs (65 miles)
✿**Tribal area elevations:** 2,400–5,200 feet
✿**Tribe established:** The Havasupai People have inhabited their tribal lands for a minimum of 800 years.
✿**Area:** 251,000 acres
✿**Annual visitation:** 12,000

⌇ Getting There:

✿**Airport:**
♦Sky Harbor Airport, Phoenix, AZ (315 miles)
♦McCarran Airport, Las Vegas, NV (220 miles)

✿**Vehicle:**
♦From I-40 eastbound in Kingman take Exit 53 and go left (north-northeast) to Andy Devine Avenue/State Route 66. Proceed 50 miles to Peach Springs. Passing Peach Springs, continue another 6 miles to

Indian Route 18. Take the left (north) onto IR 18 and proceed 60 miles to the end of the road at Hualapai Hilltop trailhead and parking area.

♦From I-40 westbound, take Exit 123 to State Route 66 Seligman/Peach Springs and drive 34 miles to Indian Route 18. Take the right (north) onto IR 18 and proceed 60 miles to the end of the road at Hualapai Hilltop trailhead and parking area.

≈ Contact:
✿**Web:** www.havasupaitribe.com
✿**Phone:** (928) 448-2121
✿**Mail:** Havasupai Tribe, P.O. Box 160, Supai, AZ 86435

≈ The Layout:
The Havasupai Tribe is reportedly the smallest Indian nation in the United States, and this hike takes place on their private tribal lands. There is no road access into Havasu Canyon or the Village of Supai. The trail is utilized by hikers, as well as the Havasupai people, who primarily employ horses on the trail to bring in supplies and transport tourists and their gear to the lodge and campground. Access can also be gained via helicopter, departing at the Hualapai Hilltop Trailhead. There is a lodge in Supai, as well as a small café, and a small but well-stocked general store (no camping gear). Havasu Campground is about two miles north of the village, just past Havasu Falls. The closest lodgings outside of the canyon are at Seligman, Peach Springs, or the Grand Canyon Caverns Inn (about 12 miles east of IR 18).

More than half of the hike to Supai is along Hualapai Canyon, a pleasant hike through a narrow gully that widens upon reaching Havasu Canyon. Always be cognizant of fast-moving horse trains heading up and down the canyon: Step off the trail and allow them unimpeded

A mare and her foal graze along the trail in Hualapai Canyon.

passage. Due to the horses, this is not a pristine trail; it is usually dusty, and always maintains the scent of horse poo. This canyon is quiet in the winter and gets very busy in spring when temperatures warm up and visitors can swim in its various pools. Summers can still be busy, but beware: Temperatures are scorching during this season, and although you can usually find shade along this trail you'll need to carry plenty of water. Make sure you are not on the trail during the hottest time of the day. In autumn the cottonwoods turn brilliant yellow, the crowds thin out, and by late November the canyon again gets nice and quiet.

The lodge is simple and clean. Rooms include two double beds, bath, and air conditioning, but no telephone, no television, no coffeemaker, and no smoking. The campground is primitive and fairly shaded. There is spring water available, some composting toilets, and a picnic table at most sites. There are no showers but creek bathing is allowed—no soaps please (including biodegradable soaps). No campfires are allowed and all trash must be packed out. Alcohol, drugs, weapons, and pets are not allowed in Havasu.

≋ Permits and Restrictions:

Accessing Havasu Canyon is not cheap. The cost for camping at the time of this writing includes an entrance fee ($35 per person), an environmental fee ($5 per person), and the campground fee ($17 per person, per night), plus tax. If you show up without a reservation, you'll be charged double on all fees. A lodge room for four (with two double beds) runs $180 per night. Day hikers too are required to check in and pay the entry and environmental fees. Make lodge reservations directly with the lodge; campground reservations are made through the Tourism Office. Gear can be packed in by horse for a fee. Campers must register and pay at the Tourism Office, while lodgers check in at the lodge. Campers are then issued a wrist bracelet, and lodgers are issued a tag to verify their registration with the tribe. Rangers regularly patrol the trail to the falls verifying that visitors have been properly registered.

During seasonal heat (late April through October) the Havasupai Tribe can, and will, close the trail completely to day hikers, deeming it too dangerous to attempt the grueling 20-mile round-trip hike to Havasu Falls and back to Hualapai Hilltop. This is due to the fact that too many day hikers have required rescue after attempting this arduous hike totally unprepared.

≋ Trail Overview:

This trail is usually done as an overnight outing. Day hiking is generally allowed (entry fee still required), but the canyon can be closed to all day hikers during seasonal heat (April–October).

⚙ **Length:** 20 miles round-trip (Hualapai Hilltop to Havasu Campground)
⚙ **Difficulty:** Easy to moderate
⚙ **Elevations:** 2,300–5,200 feet
⚙ **Hiking times:** 2–3 days
⚙ **Water availability:** No water is available at the trailhead (although there may be a vendor selling cold drinks). No dependable water is available on the trail until reaching the creek at Havasu Canyon. Creek water needs to be treated. Potable water is available in Supai and at the campground.
⚙ **Toilets:** Composting toilets at the trailhead and campground
⚙ **Special advisories:** Heat is always an issue when hiking in the warm season along the Colorado Plateau. Make sure you employ a sound heat strategy and get off the trail during the midday heat. This usually means beginning your hike before 7 a.m. during the summer season. Hiking at night is frowned upon unless you are very familiar with the trail. Listening to an MP3 player or other device is not recommended on this trail since the horses and mules moving up and down this canyon move fast and you could easily get trampled if you're unable to hear an oncoming horse train. When horse trains approach, quickly step off the trail as far as possible with everyone in your group on the same side of the trail. Do not reach out to the horses as they pass. Trail dust can aggravate those with allergies or other health concerns. Shoes with ankle coverage or low hiking gaiters can be helpful in keeping the fine silty trail sand out of your shoes. Use caution if you choose to swim near the tops of any waterfalls as the currents can be treacherous. Be sure to hang your food when not in camp and especially at night—squirrels, ravens, and raccoons are plentiful in this canyon. No rock climbing is allowed anywhere. Small dogs from the village will often follow hikers, and if you feed them they will probably stay with you throughout the trip. They appear to operate as unofficial canyon guides and companions.

≈ Trail Description:

The journey begins where the road ends at Hualapai Hilltop. Try not to be disappointed by the view from Hilltop where the rock walls are a bland green-beige-gray; after the first mile you'll be travelling inside a wonderful red rock canyon. The trailhead is located on the north end of the parking area, and toilets are to the left of the trailhead. No water is available. The first mile (and last when you return) is the toughest, as the trail drops precipitously from Hilltop along a series of switchbacks. The trail moves generally northeast, and before you know it, the trail will have descended 1,000 feet in this first mile, dropping into the dry wash of Hualapai Canyon as it curves to the right (north).

Once in the wash, you'll remain in this gradually deepening canyon for the next 6.5 miles, generally keeping to a north-northeast heading. The deeper you continue into Hualapai Canyon, the more beautiful it becomes. Always listen for the sound of horses shuttling up and down the canyon; they can come upon you quickly. When horses approach, step to the side of the trail and stay still. Traditionally, there is no word for "hello" in the Havasupais' native language, so I usually just nod to the horse wranglers as they go by. At about 6 miles from the trailhead, you will begin to see a few small springs in Hualapai Canyon, just prior to reaching Havasu Canyon and Havasu Creek. Entering Havasu Canyon, you will have traveled 6.5 miles from Hilltop.

The environment changes dramatically from Hualapai Canyon to the Havasu Canyon junction. This intersection immediately broadens out into a forested plain with the stunning blue-green water of Havasu Creek running through its midsection. Protocol mandates that from here through the Village of Supai, visitors remain on the trail. The land is privately owned by the Havasupai people inhabiting the canyon and unwelcomed intrusions could be considered trespassing.

Make sure at this canyon junction that you head left (north and slightly northwest) and that you are hiking downstream along Havasu Canyon. From the confluence, the path meanders through the riparian woodlands and crosses a small wooden bridge at about 7.25 miles.

Bathers enjoy the blue-green waters below Havasu Falls.

In less than a half-mile, you'll be entering the Village of Supai. The double rock pillars seen to the left are known as Wigleeva, they are the guardian spirits of the Havasupai people. Soon you will see a small store and grill on the left. Stay to the right after the store, and before long you'll reach the town center, a total of eight miles from Hilltop. As you pass through the center of the village, you'll easily spot the Tourist Office on the left, then the post office, café, and general store. (They are all well signed.) The lodge is around the corner from the café. If you

are staying at the lodge, you'll follow the road as it curves left past the café, turns right near the school, then proceeds straight toward the church. The church will be on your left, as you head off to the right, and then slightly left where the lodge will be just ahead.

To get to the waterfalls and campground, take the same left past the café, an immediate right, then another left at the church (signed). After leaving the village the trail soon arcs north-northeast. The number of homes will decrease and you quickly find yourself back within the riparian habitat full of willows and tall cottonwoods. Before long you will hear New Navajo Falls, and as the trail continues it will finally come into slightly obstructed view. There are a couple of not-so-obvious trails to get you over to the base of New Navajo Falls: One is dry but requires a bit of precarious scrambling, and the other low route gets you wet but offers easier access.

Past the campground is another beautiful waterfall—Mooney Falls.

Continuing on, you'll see a campground sign as the trail descends and crosses the creek via a wooden-planked bridge. Shortly thereafter you'll begin down a long series of staircase steps taking you near the base of Havasu Falls roaring off to your right (east). It is a striking waterfall plunging nearly 100 feet into the deep blue-green pool below. As the trail levels out you'll see a path to the right that will take you to the water's edge in front of Havasu Falls.

Just downstream of Havasu Falls the campground suddenly appears, a mere ten miles from where you began at the trailhead. There is plenty of shade. The creek flows through the campground's sites, and there are usually plenty of campsites to choose from. The campground has composting toilets, and there is potable spring water available. You are allowed to bath in the creek (no soaps, please), but be mindful of the current. In 2010 a man who was swimming in the creek above Mooney Falls died after being swept over the 200-foot waterfall.

The hike gets even better and more adventurous as you continue downstream to Mooney Falls and Beaver Falls. Mooney Falls, another breathtaking sight, is just past the last campsite and requires a moderately precarious downclimb through rough tunnels, chain-assisted verticals, and finally a couple of rickety ladders. It's not as difficult as it may sound, and the awesome view of the falls from the bottom is well worth the effort. As you forge ahead you'll have to get your feet wet a few times when the trail crisscrosses the stream, but about 2.5 miles from Mooney Falls, you'll see the impressive cascades of Beaver Falls.

The majority of people turn around here, but the trail does continue another four miles, crossing into Grand Canyon National Park and emerging from the canyon at Havasu Rapids along the mighty Colorado River. Occasionally you will see river runners hiking upstream in their flip-flops heading into the village for supplies.

Havasu Canyon trail, like so many others, returns to the real world along the same route. So spend time frolicking and feeling the mist of the falls before hiking back to Hilltop while reminiscing about the gleaming turquoise streams, tall cottonwood trees, and falling waters of the paradise you just experienced.

⌇ Mileage Log from the Trailhead:
- ✿**Hualapai Canyon wash:** 1 mile
- ✿**Havasu Canyon:** 6.5 miles
- ✿**Supai Village:** 8 miles
- ✿**New Navajo Falls:** 9.5 miles
- ✿**Havasu Falls:** 9.8 miles
- ✿**Havasu Campground:** 10 miles
- ✿**Mooney Falls:** 10.5 miles
- ✿**Beaver Falls:** 13 miles
- ✿**Colorado River:** 18.5 miles

⌇ Other Area Trails and Attractions:

✿**Grand Canyon National Park:** Take your choice between multiple drop-dead gorgeous trails.

✿**San Francisco Peaks (Flagstaff, Arizona):** To climb the tallest mountain in Arizona, take the trail from the Arizona Snowbowl Ski and Snowboard Resort to the top of Humphrey's Peak (12,637 feet).

✿**Sedona, Arizona:** A hiker's Mecca, Sedona is another beautiful area filled with exquisite red rock canyons and formations, with a large number of trails to choose from, including West Fork Trail (described on page 112).

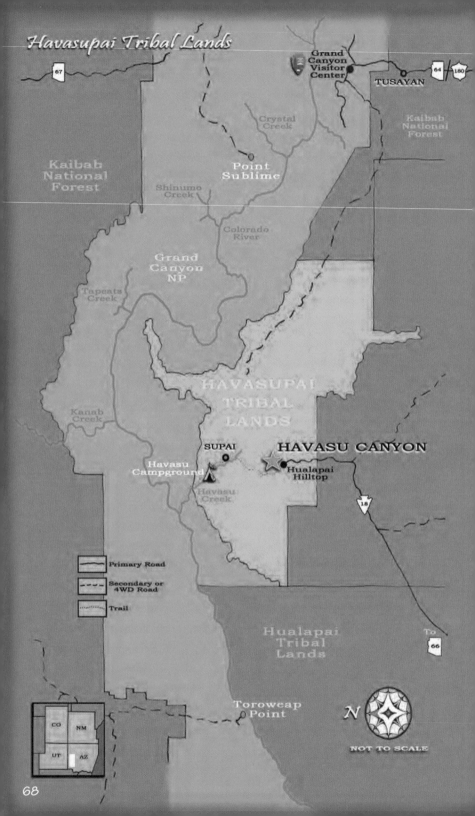

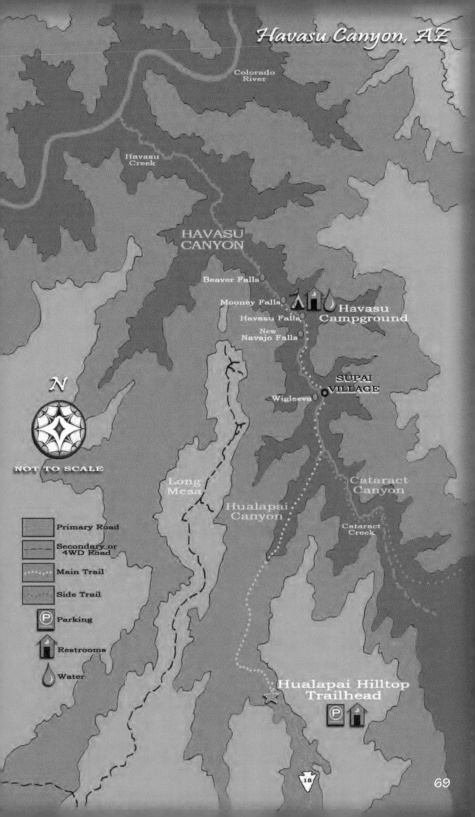

Havasu Canyon, AZ

Colorado River

Havasu Creek

HAVASU CANYON

Beaver Falls

Mooney Falls

Havasu Falls

New Navajo Falls

Havasu Campground

SUPAI VILLAGE

Wigleeva

N

NOT TO SCALE

Long Mesa

Hualapai Canyon

Cataract Canyon

Cataract Creek

Primary Road

Secondary or 4WD Road

Main Trail

Side Trail

P Parking

Restrooms

Water

Hualapai Hilltop Trailhead

P

18

69

The first migrants to cross the Bering Land Bridge entered North America sometime between 15,000 and 17,000 years ago. The oldest known evidence suggests that human population along the Colorado Plateau began during the Paleoindian Period around 11,000 B.C. These were nomadic people who moved around the region following and hunting large game. This period was also marked by an environment that was significantly cooler and wetter.

Cultural and environmental changes began during the Archaic Period, 9,000–2,000 B.C. This was a time of warmer temperatures and occasional droughts. The inhabitants of canyon country were still hunter-gatherer cultures, but these foraging societies started forming defined territories anchored to places where they had begun relying more on agriculture and long-term food storage. By the Late Archaic Age (2,000 B.C.–A.D. 200) agriculture was being introduced to the plateau, quickly transforming the culture and further enhancing notions of place and community.

Between A.D. 200 and 1250, as agricultural productivity grew, so did the population. Thus, the farming civilizations of the Ancestral Puebloan (Anasazi) and Fremont cultures emerged. The Ancient Puebloans were the first inhabitants along the plateau to adopt many crops, such as corn, beans, and squash. They grew cotton and made clothing from its fibers, and they were the first to build water reservoirs and develop large cities. Their excellent basket-making skills eventually developed into pottery making.

As the Anasazi evolved, the Fremont people also rose to prominence. For the most part, the Ancestral Puebloans inhabited the southern areas of the plateau, especially the Four Corners region, while the Fremont lived in the northern areas and into the Great Basin to the west. Little is known about the Fremont peoples. It appears they were a mixture of farmers and hunter-gatherers, but they didn't build large home sites or cities as did the Ancestral Puebloans.

Although these two cultures shared many of the same tools and crafts, it is unknown how they interacted with each other. Combined, these two cultures probably numbered more people than those who live in this same region today. To feed all those people, they utilized nearly every available space toward the industry of growing crops. Trying to support agriculture in such an inhospitable and varying climate inevitably created an atmosphere of conflict between those with surplus and those with little.

Partly due to both environmental and societal stresses, both cultures gradually faded between the years 1250 and 1500. Contributing factors include extended drought and climate change, soil erosion and depletion, and raids by other communities. The people abandoned their homes, never moved back, and reportedly returned to a more mobile hunter-gatherer society.

The 1500s brought the first European exploration into the region, introducing a multitude of diseases for which the native populations had no natural resistance. In the resulting population vacuum, the remaining people, along with immigrants from other areas of the Southwest, formed the essence of the region's modern tribes, among them the Northern Paiute, Shoshone, Navajo, Hopi, and the Ute-Southern Paiute tribes.

Repeated epidemics and conflicts within their own tribes and with European explorers shaped the plateau, and by the time American settlers entered the area, these conflicts only increased. Euro-American bigotry and racial hatred, coupled with unadulterated exploitation and occupation of native lands, caused further strife for the indigenous populations. Tribes were ultimately deceived, decimated, displaced, and disenfranchised.

By the nineteenth and twentieth centuries these same Native Americans, nearly destroyed by cultural genocide and Manifest Destiny, entered into the realm of myth and lore. The romantic image of the proud Native American on horseback, wielding his hunting spear, still reigns in our American culture, while in reality many of these first, true Americans still struggle with the changes that were forced upon them.

Antelope House Ruins, Canyon de Chelly National Monument, was abandoned around 1250. Earlier pit houses found beneath these ruins date back to A.D. 700.

Hermit Trail
Grand Canyon National Park
Arizona

≋ Claim to Fame:

While the Grand Canyon is not quite the deepest in the world, it is by far the most visually spectacular. One mile deep and up to 18 miles wide, the canyon has been cut layer by colorful layer by erosive forces to expose this geologically striated wonderland. Its immensity is difficult to appraise, as it can overwhelm the senses to gaze across its vast expanse. A hike from rim to river provides the canyon explorer with a sense of its geological history, as it illustrates how the powerful Colorado River and its tributaries slowly carved its walls down into some of the lowest layers of exposed rock on the face of the earth.

This hike, drenched in history, takes you on the spectacular and challenging Hermit Trail to Granite Rapids, one of the most picturesque areas of whitewater and sandy beach on the Colorado River. As you descend steeply over 4,000 feet from rim to river, you'll pass through conifer forest, pinyon-juniper woodland, desert scrub, and riparian ecosystems. Not for the novice Grand Canyon hiker, this trail provides a true wilderness experience inside the most majestic of all southwest canyons.

≋ Park Overview:
○ **Closest town**: Tusayan, AZ (3 miles)
○ **Park elevations:** 2,400–7,000 feet
○ **Park established:** January 11, 1908 (NM), February 26, 1919 (NP)
○ **Area:** 1,218,375 acres
○ **Annual visitation**: 4,388,386

≋ Getting There (GCNP, South Rim):
○ **Airport:**
♦ Sky Harbor Airport, Phoenix, AZ (232 miles)
♦ McCarran Airport, Las Vegas, NV (274 miles)
♦ Grand Canyon Airport, Tusayan, AZ (6 miles)

○ **Vehicle:**
♦ From I-40 (AZ), take Exit 165 (Williams, Grand Canyon) to State Route 64 and drive 60 miles to the south entrance of Grand Canyon National Park.

♦ From US Route 89, turn west onto State Route 64 in Cameron, AZ. Drive 35 miles to the east entrance of Grand Canyon National Park.

≋ Contact:
○ **Web:** www.nps.gov/grca
○ **Phone:** (928) 638-7888 (General Information), or (928) 638-7875 (Backcountry Information Center: Calls are only taken from 1 p.m.–5 p.m. Monday–Friday.)
○ **Mail:** Grand Canyon NP, P.O. Box 129, Grand Canyon, AZ 86023

ᨁ **The Layout**:

The developed areas of Grand Canyon National Park consist of two varied and widely separated areas—the South Rim and the North Rim. The South Rim has better views, more inner canyon trails, and is more accessible and therefore by far the most visited. On the other hand, the North Rim is quiet, secluded, quaint, a bit cooler, and is less accessible, as well as being closed during the winter months. Hermit Trail leaves from the South Rim. The best times to hike into the canyon are spring and fall. Winters are cool to cold, and summers are, literally, "killer" desert heat for anyone venturing into the lower elevations of the canyon's inner gorge.

Most of the canyon's annual visitation is during the summer when temperatures along the rim are moderate, but when temperatures within the inner canyon are about 20 degrees hotter. The classic rim-to-rim trips into the canyon take place along the cross-canyon or "Corridor" trails (Bright Angel, South Kaibab, and North Kaibab trails). These trails are by far the most popular trails going into the canyon. They are the only maintained trails, and are easily followed.

ᨁ **Permits and Restrictions**:

Permits are required for any overnight trip into the Grand Canyon, (unless you've made reservations at Phantom Ranch), and demand is high. Applications are accepted five months in advance, and although walk-in permits may be available, walk-in applications are not accepted during the first thirty days that permits are available. Permit applications should

Granite Rapids is one of the most picturesque settings along the mighty Colorado River.

be mailed to arrive on the first of the month, or faxed (highly recommended) on the first day of the month, four months prior to the proposed start month. For example, if you want to hike in April, you would apply on December 1. During the trip, your permit must be in your possession and should be displayed in plain view when camped.

♒ Trail Overview:

This trail description is from Hermits Rest Trailhead to Granite Rapids. Portions of this trail can be done as a day hike, but it is *highly* recommended that any rim-to-river-to-rim hike in the Grand Canyon be done as an overnight backpack trip.

☼**Length:** 10.5 miles
☼**Difficulty:** Very difficult and strenuous!
☼**Elevations:** Hermits Rest (6,650 feet) to Colorado River (2,400 feet) 4,250 feet total change
☼**Day-hike destinations:** Dripping Springs, Santa Maria Springs
☼**Hiking times:** 8 hours from Hermits Rest to Granite Rapids
☼**Water availability:** Hermits Rest, Santa Maria Springs (unreliable), Dripping Springs (2 miles west of Hermit Trail), Hermit Creek (1 mile west along the Tonto Trail), and the Colorado River. Water from all wilderness sources, including Santa Maria Springs, should be treated before drinking.
☼**Toilets:** Toilets are available at Hermits Rest.
☼**Special advisories:** This is an unmaintained trail. Advanced route-finding skills are required (mostly due to the numerous rock slides), and temperatures rise, on average, twenty degrees from the rim to the river, with summer temps frequently exceeding 110 degrees in the shade. It is highly recommended that first-time hikers going into the Grand Canyon choose to hike along the cross-corridor trails to gain insight and experience for hiking in this extreme environment.

As the park service warns, "A hike into the Grand Canyon will test your physical and mental endurance." Hermit Trail is steep and exposed. If you plan on hiking in the summer season, make sure you are off the trail between the hottest hours of the day, between about 9 a.m. and 4 p.m. This is a beautiful hike, taking you into the vast and harsh Grand Canyon. It makes you work hard to experience its spectacular landscape, but it is so well worth it!

♒ Trailhead Directions:

From the South Entrance Road, head west toward the rim lodges, passing El Tovar and Bright Angel Lodge, where you'll soon spot Hermit Road (on right and gated). Hermit Road is accessed only by shuttle bus from March 1 to November 30, with buses running from 7:30 a.m.

to one hour after sunset. Otherwise, if you are going to the trailhead at a time when shuttles are not running, ask at the Backcountry Information Center for the access code to the gate. The keypad is attached to the steel post at the entry gate. The end of Hermit Road is called Hermits Rest. From the paved loop at Hermits Rest, you'll see a gravel service road heading right (west) from the restrooms; drive to the end of the road and the trailhead parking area. The trailhead begins at the opening along the middle of the wooden post fence, and there is a Park Service trailhead kiosk adjacent to the trail.

≈ Trail Description:

The trail begins in a general west to southwest direction and is relatively easy to follow through the juniper and pine woodland. It starts off steep, with varying long and short switchbacks. There are many little side trails, especially near the top, so pay attention. If you find you've left the trail, simply backtrack until you regain the main trail. After about 100 feet of descent, you'll find yourself heading north-northwest for a stint, dropping about 300 feet to an unnamed point where you gain some nice views into the canyon before getting back to a south-southwest heading. Occasionally, you'll find yourself walking on cobblestone sections, remnants of the original trail. Hermit Basin will soon come into view. After traversing along the eastern rim of the basin, a series of switchbacks will take you down into the basin. At 1.4 miles from the trailhead, you'll see the Waldron Trail junction on the left (south).

Passing this first trail junction, you'll be heading west. Soon the trail curves toward the north as you drop another 200 feet to the junction with the Dripping Springs/Boucher Trail. This marks a total descent so far of nearly 1,400 feet in about 1.6 miles. Stay north as you enter a normally dry wash, staying to the left (west) and getting back on the trail soon after entering the wash. Before long you'll be at the headwall of Hermit Gorge, referred to as Red Top, where you get one of the first expansive views into this long side canyon. After dropping down a few quick switchbacks and crossing a lower section of the same dry wash you crossed above, you will begin the lengthy traverse along the east side of the canyon. From this point downward, the trail begins to get decidedly more difficult, and you will see less pinyon pine and juniper as the vegetation begins to change to desert scrub brush.

At 2.2 miles from the rim, you reach the popular day-hike destination named Santa Maria Spring and its accompanying resthouse. The spring itself is a pipe emptying into the trough next to the shelter. This water is normally flowing but is considered unreliable, especially in the midst of a dry early summer. Also important to note: This water should be treated before drinking. The shelter is a nice respite from the sun, and last time I visited, it had a double rocking chair and a wooden bench to allow a bit of relaxation before moving on.

From the spring, you'll continue the long traverse in a generally northeast direction with occasional switchback descents, but all told, from the spring to Cathedral Stairs, there is only about a 600-foot drop in elevation. About a mile from the spring, you'll enter a large gully cutting in toward the east where you'll encounter the first of four major rock slides. Take care crossing these slide areas as the footing may be loose and precipitous. Make sure you look ahead and pay attention to cairns and other trail signs to ensure that once you've crossed the slide area you return onto the trail. Shortly after passing a second rock slide area you'll encounter a minor overlook that has been referred to as Panorama Point. Past that point you'll begin the steep and quick descent northwest to Lookout Point. This point is a small reddish-brown butte about 4.5 miles from the trailhead and provides another opportunity to take a break.

Moving on from Lookout Point, the hiking moderates for about three-quarters of a mile. You'll soon encounter a couple more rock-slides; the worst is where the trail curves back to the west just prior to Breezy Point. Again, take your time through the slide areas; cairns and sandy footprints from previous hikers will help show you the way. From Breezy Point, a quick canyon stroll takes you to the top of Cathedral Stairs and one of the best canyon views, looking northeast across a saddle along the spine of Cope Butte.

Cathedral Stairs is a series of over two dozen tight switchbacks of loosening rock. The stairs drop about 400 feet to a long descending traverse along the talus slope of Cope Butte. This is the last big descent, a nearly 1,300 foot drop from the top of the stairs to the Tonto Trail junction. Most of the stairs are in pretty good shape, save for a section near the top where loose rock and toppled remnants of the original cobblestone and concrete litter the trail. Completing the descent of the Cope Butte traverse, a series of lesser switchbacks will take you down to the next trail sign at the junction of Hermit and Tonto Trails. This junction is just about 6.7 miles from Hermit's Rest.

At the Hermit/Tonto junction you'll want to go right (northeast), climbing up toward a small saddle. After the lengthy descent, it's nice to be able walk on semi-level ground. The other option is to go left (southwest) toward Hermit Creek if

The Monument

you will be camping at Hermit Rapids or Hermit Creek Camp. Reaching the saddle, you gain a beautiful view down a side gorge to the Colorado River. The trail from here heads northeast and slowly wends its way around the tip of Cope Butte, curving east. As the trail continues around to the south, you'll begin looking down into Monument Creek Gorge. Continue moving south toward the head of the tributary canyon, and the trail will eventually turn back to the northeast and along a narrow ledge until you get to the Monument.

You'll soon see a sign where the Tonto Trail meets the Monument Creek Trail. The Monument is a rock pinnacle rising some 200 feet near the trail junction, and therefore it's pretty difficult to miss. Take the side trail of loose rock and steep switchbacks down into Monument Creek Gorge. This side canyon quickly meets up with the main canyon, and you follow the wash downstream (north), toward the Colorado River. The trail stays mainly in the wash, occasionally crossing back along the overland sides of the creek to cut corners. After about 1.5 miles in Monument Creek wash, you'll begin to hear the roar of the Colorado River, emerging from the drainage just above Granite Rapids.

The best campsites are to the right (east) along the beach, but there are plenty of places on both sides of Monument Creek to make camp. It is very important that you store your food immediately, and in a manner that does not allow the various critters access: Hang your food bag, or utilize some other form of chew-proof container or sack to prevent such thievery. Given half the chance, they will eat all your food. After spending time at Granite Rapids, you can return to the South Rim via the same route or utilize the other trail options listed below.

⁓ Trail Options:
Spending the night at Hermit Camp (7 miles from Hermits Rest) is always a nice option. Better yet, make this trip into a gorgeous semi-loop by heading east along the Tonto Trail to Indian Garden before the hike out along Bright Angel Trail (although permits for Indian Garden can be more difficult to obtain).

⁓ Mileage Log from the Trailhead (6,650 feet):
- ✿ **Waldron Trail junction:** 1.4 miles, (5,430 feet)
- ✿ **Dripping Springs/Boucher Trail junction:** 1.6 miles, (5,220 feet)
- ✿ **Santa Maria Springs:** 2.2 miles, (4,960 feet)
- ✿ **Lookout Point:** 4.5 miles, (4,569 feet)
- ✿ **Top of Cathedral Stairs:** 6.1 miles, (4,430 feet)
- ✿ **Hermit-Tonto Trail junction:** 6.7 miles, (3,210 feet)
- ✿ **Monument Creek junction:** 8.9 miles, (2,850 feet)
- ✿ **Granite Rapids (Colorado River):** 10.5 miles, (2,400 feet)

Prickly pear cactus bloom along Tonto Trail.

⁀ Trail History:

This trail was built in 1911 by the Santa Fe Railroad to fuel the thriving tourist industry in and around the Grand Canyon. At the time, it was a state-of-the-art trail, most of which was constructed with thousands of hand-fitted rocks that created a smooth cobblestone surface. The remnants can still be found along a few stretches of the trail today. Ten years before Phantom Ranch was built, Hermit Camp was seen as the ultimate in canyon luxury accommodations, including a tramway from the rim, an automobile for facility transport, and its own chef. The original Hermit Camp closed in 1930, but a few of the old foundations can still be found near the present-day Hermit Creek primitive campground.

Hermit Trail is named after prospector Louis D. Boucher, who came to the canyon around 1890. He built the nearby Dripping Springs and Boucher Trails and lived in the canyon area for twenty years, maintaining seasonal residences at Dripping Springs and near Boucher Creek. Although he was called a hermit because he lived alone, he was by many accounts quite sociable and a gracious host whenever tourists would stop by.

⁀ Other Area Trails and Attractions:

✿**South Kaibab Trail (South Rim):** This is a classic Grand Canyon hiking experience along one of the popular corridor trails. South Kaibab Trail provides some of the most outstanding open vistas found in the park.

✿**Thunder River Trail and Deer Creek (North Rim):** This difficult trail off the North Rim takes you to Thunder River, the shortest river in the world, as it comes bursting forth from the canyon's wall. Deer Creek Falls is the other lovely attraction for this hike.

✿**Havasu Canyon:** Located to the west of the National Park, this hike enters the home of the Havasupai Tribe. The canyon contains a few of the most resplendent waterfalls in the American Southwest. See details for this hike on page 60.

✿**Little Colorado River Gorge:** This gorge rivals some of my favorite hikes, although many of its diverse and spectacular areas, such as Blue Springs, are rarely discussed or visited. Though information about hiking this area is sparse, it is well worth your time researching, planning, and exploring this beautiful gorge.

✿**Sedona, Arizona:** Sedona is a beautiful area of exquisite red rock canyons and formations, with a large number of trails to choose from, including West Fork Trail, described on page 112.

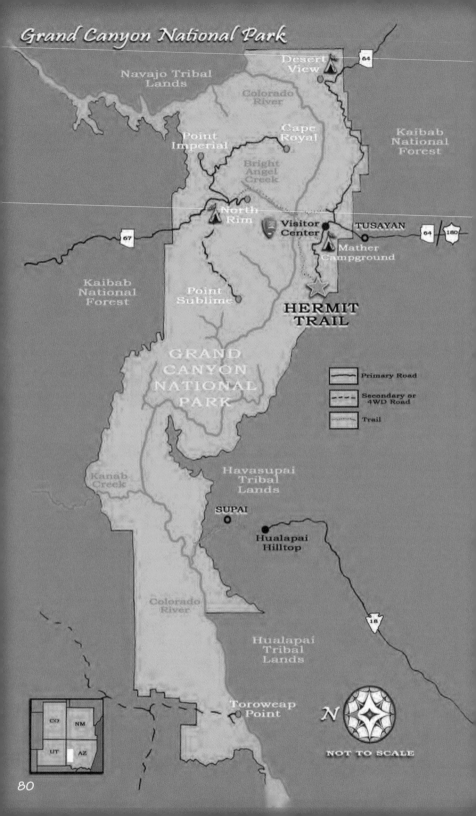

Grand Canyon National Park

Navajo Tribal Lands

Colorado River

Kaibab National Forest

Point Imperial

Cape Royal

Bright Angel Creek

North Rim

Visitor Center

TUSAYAN

Mather Campground

HERMIT TRAIL

Point Sublime

Kaibab National Forest

GRAND CANYON NATIONAL PARK

	Primary Road
	Secondary or 4WD Road
	Trail

Desert View

Havasupai Tribal Lands

SUPAI

Hualapai Hilltop

Kanab Creek

Colorado River

Hualapai Tribal Lands

Toroweap Point

N

NOT TO SCALE

CO NM UT AZ

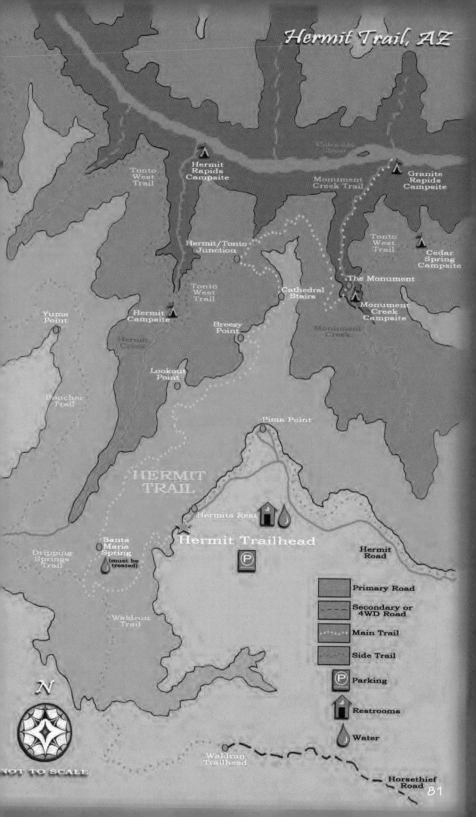

The Narrows

Zion National Park

Utah

⁓ Claim to Fame:

Massive canyon walls colored cream to pink to reddish-brown enclose visitors venturing into the heart of Zion National Park. Zion Canyon is over 16 miles long, a deeply cut gorge that is continuously made deeper as its silty sediments are carried away by the North Fork of the Virgin River. The park contains four unique ecosystems, including desert, creeks, woodlands, and conifer forests, and holds a multitude of choices for hikers and backpackers to enjoy the magnificent backcountry and wilderness.

The Zion Narrows hiking trail is the most popular hike in the park, although a majority of visitors travel along the paved Riverside Walk only to the point about a mile upstream where the asphalt ends. To continue on and hike the Narrows, plan on getting wet; the majority of the hike is in the cool flowing waters of the North Fork of the Virgin River. Silt accumulating on the submerged river rock makes river crossings very slick, and using hiking staffs to help keep you on your feet is highly recommended. Hiking in the Narrows has often been described as walking on greasy bowling balls. The Narrows is a drop-dead gorgeous canyon with walls closing down to only 20 feet wide and soaring up to 2,000 feet high, while boasting lush green riparian islands around every corner. You are sure to find the Narrows one of the most splendid canyon hikes in the world.

⁓ Park Overview:

○ **Closest town:** Springdale, UT (directly outside the park's south entrance)
○ **Park elevations:** 3,666–8,726 feet
○ **Park established:** July 31, 1909
○ **Area:** 146,597 acres
○ **Annual visitation:** 2,665,972

⁓ Getting There:

○ **Airport:**
♦ Salt Lake City Airport, Salt Lake City, UT (310 miles)
♦ McCarran Airport, Las Vegas, NV (170 miles)
♦ Saint George Municipal Airport, St. George, UT (50 miles)
♦ Cedar City Regional Airport, Cedar City, UT (60 miles)

○ **Vehicle:**
♦ From I-15 southbound, take Exit 27 to State Route 17, driving south for 26 miles. At La Verkin, take a left (east) onto SR 9 and travel 21 miles to Zion National Park Visitor Center on the right.

♦ From I-15 northbound, take Exit 16 to State Route 9 east, driving 33 miles. At La Verkin, take a right to remain on SR 9 and travel 21 miles to Zion National Park Visitor Center on the right.

◆From US 89, turn west onto State Route 9 (the Zion–Mount Carmel Highway) at Mount Carmel Junction, Utah, and proceed 36 miles to the Zion National Park Visitor Center on the left.

≈≈ Contact:
☼**Web:** www.nps.gov/zion
☼**Phone:** (435) 772-3256
☼**Mail:** Zion National Park, Springdale, UT 84767

≈≈ The Layout:
Though Zion National Park is a relatively small park in size, it is high in visitation with nearly 3 million annual visitors, and it contains three rather distinct hiking areas. The main valley is Zion Canyon. It is overwhelmingly the most popular area in the park, containing some of the premier hiking destinations inside a breathtakingly beautiful and majestic canyon. Another good hiking region lies along Kolob Terrace Road (off SR 9) as it weaves in and out of the park to the west-northwest of Zion Canyon. This part of Kolob Terrace Road provides access to some wonderful, quiet trails along the Lower Kolob Plateau. The third region is Kolob Canyons, even further to the northwest of Zion Canyon. Accessed from I-15, Kolob Canyon Road is the starting point for several of the best hikes outside of Zion Canyon.

The higher elevations of this park can make summers slightly more bearable than elsewhere, but temperatures can still exceed 100 degrees in the shade inside low-lying Zion Canyon. Remember too that this popular canyon has the inherent danger of flash floods during summer thunderstorms. Spring and fall are the most popular times for backcountry exploration but yield a wide variety of weather conditions. Winter is usually cold and wet; roads are plowed, but trails may be closed due to the slippery conditions.

Zion Lodge, the only lodging inside the park, includes a more formal dining room. Casual dining is available seasonally at the Castle Dome Café adjacent to the lodge. Fuel and plentiful food and lodging choices are located just outside the park's south entrance in Springdale, Utah. Outfitters in Springdale also rent water shoes and cold water gear

A tranquil setting inside the Narrows.

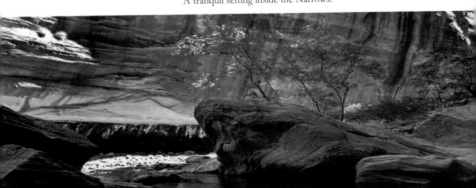

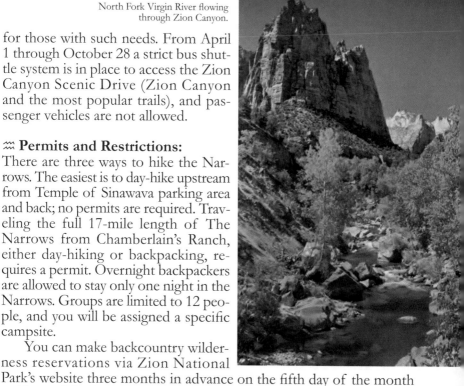

North Fork Virgin River flowing through Zion Canyon.

for those with such needs. From April 1 through October 28 a strict bus shuttle system is in place to access the Zion Canyon Scenic Drive (Zion Canyon and the most popular trails), and passenger vehicles are not allowed.

ᔧ Permits and Restrictions:

There are three ways to hike the Narrows. The easiest is to day-hike upstream from Temple of Sinawava parking area and back; no permits are required. Traveling the full 17-mile length of The Narrows from Chamberlain's Ranch, either day-hiking or backpacking, requires a permit. Overnight backpackers are allowed to stay only one night in the Narrows. Groups are limited to 12 people, and you will be assigned a specific campsite.

You can make backcountry wilderness reservations via Zion National Park's website three months in advance on the fifth day of the month at 10 a.m. If no permit has been secured in advance, visitors can also garner a permit online through Zion's last-minute drawing reservation system. Otherwise, some walk-in permits are made available each morning at the Visitor Center Wilderness Desk beginning at 7 a.m. the day prior to your hike. A reservation is not a permit; the actual permit is issued upon checking in at the visitor center. Fees are based on group size: $10 for 1 or 2 people, $15 for 3–7, and $20 for 8–12 people. The park service will close the canyon and cancel your trip at any time if it is determined that there is an increased risk of a flash flood. Visit the Zion National Park website (www.nps.gov/zion/planyourvisit/zion-backcountry-information.htm) for more detailed information.

ᔧ Trail Overview:

This trail can be done as a day hike from Temple of Sinawava parking area. Hiking the full length can be done as a very long day hike or an overnight backpack trip from Chamberlain's Ranch.

✿**Length:** 17 miles from Chamberlain's Ranch to Temple of Sinawava parking area.

✿**Difficulty:** Easy to moderate day hike, moderate to strenuous overnight backpack outing.

✿**Elevations:** 4,425–5,820 feet

✿**Day-hike destination:** Big Springs is the furthest recommended day-hike destination (nearly 11 miles round-trip).

○**Hiking time:** Approximately 13 hours from Chamberlain's Ranch to the Temple of Sinawava parking area

○**Water availability:** Yes, at Temple of Sinawava Trailhead. Otherwise, you'll be in the river most of the time, so pull it, treat it, and drink as much as you need.

○**Toilets:** Toilets are available at Temple of Sinawava parking area, but there are no facilities at the Chamberlain's Ranch Trailhead.

○**Special advisories:** Flash floods have killed hikers exploring this trail in the past, so make sure you check with the park service before entering the Narrows. If the water level suddenly rises, or you hear or see water rushing into the canyon, immediately climb up as fast and as far as you can: Never attempt to outrun a flash flood. Human waste systems are required (and supplied by the park service) for those venturing overnight. Packs should be waterproofed as much as possible, including camera gear. Good sturdy hiking or water shoes that cover your toes and offer ankle protection should be worn; open-toe shoes and sandals are not recommended. Using at least one hiking stick is recommended for keeping your balance on slippery river rock. Be prepared to field

 Side Step: Rock Art

Due mainly to its dry climate, the Colorado Plateau contains a huge number of surviving rock art sites. Rock art refers to the carvings (petroglyphs) and paintings (pictographs) on rock surfaces produced by Native Americans beginning many thousands of years ago. More rarely, you may encounter intaglios, which were generally larger images

created by clearing a dark-colored rock surface, thus exposing a lighter colored layer below.

Most designs consist of human and animal-like forms, but they may also include more abstract interpretations of natural icons. Please be considerate; do not mar or even touch these artworks, as the oil on your skin can speed deterioration. Feel free to take photos, make sketches (not "rubbings"), and appreciate these ancient works of art. These images have survived thousands of years, and with your help, they will be around in another thousand years.

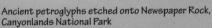
Ancient petroglyphs etched onto Newspaper Rock, Canyonlands National Park

clean your water filter due to the large amount of sediment in the river. Dry suits are available for rent in Springdale for those wanting to hike in the cooler season when the canyon's waters can be 50 degrees or below. The best months for hiking the Narrows are May, early June, September, and October, when the water is warm enough that you may not need a wetsuit, and flash flood danger is minimal. When checking water flows, bear in mind that water running through the Narrows at about 200 cfs (cubic feet per second) can be difficult to navigate, while flows over 300 cfs are considered dangerous. For a sense of wilderness solitude in summer make sure, if you are day hiking up from the Temple of Sinawava parking area, to be on the trail by 9 a.m. By the time you turn around you'll begin meeting up with the droves of people hiking, swimming, and basking inside this beautiful canyon.

≈ Trailhead Directions:

There are two ways to access to the Narrows. The first and easiest way to experience the canyon is to day hike up river from the end of the Riverside Walk. From April to October, private vehicles are not allowed admittance to the Zion Canyon Scenic Drive; all entry is via the free shuttle bus system originating at the visitor center. Take the shuttle all the way up to the Temple of Sinawava parking area at the end of the scenic drive. The obvious trailhead is signed and heads north from the parking lot.

From November to March, the Zion Canyon Scenic Drive is open to private vehicles. To get to the Riverside Walk, you'll drive north-northeast along Zion Canyon Scenic Drive, past Zion Lodge, continuing all the way to the Temple of Sinawava parking area at the end of the road.

The second access point is outside the park and starts at the Chamberlain's Ranch Trailhead. This route is used by those who are through-hiking or overnight backpacking the

Towering walls inside the Narrows.

full length of the Narrows. Since this trailhead is nearly 35 miles and one-and-a half hours drive from Zion Lodge, you'll need to hire a shuttle service to drop you off, or use two vehicles to shuttle yourselves.

To get to Chamberlain's Ranch, drive east on SR 9 and continue 2.5 miles after leaving the park's east entrance. Take a left (north) onto the North Fork Road. In about 5 miles the pavement will end; proceed on this unmaintained, rough dirt road another 12.5 miles, until it crosses a bridge over the North Fork of the Virgin River, then turn left at the next T junction and drive a quarter-mile to the main gate at Chamberlain's Ranch. Enter and make sure you close the gate behind you. This road is impassable when wet even if you are driving a 4WD vehicle; passenger cars are not advised under any conditions. A list of private shuttle companies is available from the folks manning the Visitor Center Wilderness Desk. Even on the trailhead shuttle, if the road is wet you may be given the choice of getting out and starting your hike early or turning back with the shuttle. I know, as it happened one September to me and my friends, adding about five more miles to our hike.

≋ Trail Description:

From the Chamberlain Ranch parking and shuttle drop-off area, head west-southwest, crossing the river. Follow the first few easy miles along the dirt road, but remember you are hiking on private property. Do not disturb the area as you pass through. Stay on the trail, do not collect wood for walking sticks, and do not defecate on the land or otherwise abuse the privilege of being allowed on private property. (I met the owner on one occasion as he drove up on his ATV and greeted us. We found him to be genuine and congenial.)

After hiking about 3 miles, you'll see what remains of the old Bulloch's Cabin just off the trail to the left (south-southeast). Soon after you pass the cabin, the road will end. There are several paths, but they all eventually lead into the streambed. You may put it off as long as you can, but sooner or later you'll have to enter the North Fork of the Virgin River (*aka* the North Fork) to continue on. The canyon quickly constricts as you slip into an insignificant stone crack and enter this tight-walled chasm. From here on, travel is almost exclusively in the river with intermittent land crossings on benches that shortcut back to the streambed. It is difficult to get lost from here, as long as you follow the stream flow downriver.

As you continue on, the canyon walls as well as the water level grow higher, and a little less than six miles from the trailhead you'll encounter the first official "narrows." About ten minutes beyond the National Park boundary maker (not easy to spot), you'll pass what used to be the first campsite, off to your left. This site is no longer in use and is slowly being reclaimed by nature. In another 250 yards, at about seven miles, you will reach a 12-foot waterfall flowing over a sandstone ledge. In order to skirt the waterfall, you'll want to stay left (south) and hike up the steep, well defined path. Less than a mile after the waterfall (7.5 miles total), you reach campsite number one, the Deep Creek site. The site is on the right, prior to reaching the confluence with Deep Creek, coming in from the right (north-northwest). Campsites are marked with 3-foot yellow stakes with the site number at the top; make sure to camp in your designated spot.

This is roughly the halfway point in terms of mileage from the trailhead. The water level rises here as Deep Creek increases the volume in the North Fork by nearly two-thirds, and your pace slows a bit due to the deeper water. The next campsites appear in fairly rapid succession, with camps 2–6 situated on the right side of the river. Pay close attention if one of these sites is yours: The signs are small, and having to backtrack usually isn't much fun.

Narrow Kolob Creek soon enters the canyon from the right (northwest) at nearly 10.5 miles from the trailhead, between campsites 5 and 6. Kolob Canyon is an interesting side canyon. If you are staying overnight close by, you may want to consider a quick jaunt up this pretty tributary. Campsite 7 is a few minutes past Kolob Creek, on a high bench to the left, with site number 8 across the river. Next is campsite 9, on the left and easily missed. Continuing on, Goose Creek soon enters, also on the right (west), at 11.5 miles. It is another canyon worth exploring if you have the time; otherwise you'll continue on downstream. After the Goose Creek confluence, campsite 10 is around the corner on the right, and beyond it campsite 11 and 12 (the southernmost sites) are both on the left. A mere 300 yards from campsite 12

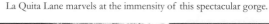

La Quita Lane marvels at the immensity of this spectacular gorge.

The Narrows with Mystery Falls far in the distance.

you arrive at Big Springs, a cascading eight-foot spring flowing from the canyon's wall. This is a beautiful spring, with pristine water creating a multilevel hanging garden. All the campsites are behind you now, so if you've missed your camp, you'll have to turn around to locate it.

From Big Springs, you'll have traveled about 12.25 miles, and soon you'll find yourself entering deeper waters with dramatic vertical walls reaching 2,000 feet high. In some places the canyon is only twenty feet wide, offering little protection from flash floods. The potential risk of flash flooding makes this the most dangerous section of the Narrows, since there is little or no high ground from here on out. Water levels are higher too, and you can expect to enter areas where the water is chest high. I lost a camera to the high water in this section when I stepped into an eddy. Although I had my camera and bag clenched in my teeth, the water came up just high enough to curl over the lip of the camera bag, and I heard the camera make some disquieting electrical crackling sounds as it quickly died of water immersion.

At about 14.5 total miles, Orderville Canyon comes in from the left (east). Orderville Canyon is another wonderful slot to explore and includes the famous sculpted tunnel of the Subway, but be aware that technical canyoneering skills are required to pass Veiled Falls, just over a half-mile up canyon. Novice hikers have broken their legs attempting to jump the falls. Continuing down the Narrows, the deepest pools are yet to come as you forge downstream, but you'll also be passing through some of the canyon's most diverse terrain, including boulder fields, riverside benches of diverse plant life, and more hanging gardens. One of the narrowest sections along this stretch is often referred to as Wall Street. From here you'll begin to encounter more day hikers up from the Temple of Sinawava parking lot. It is a motivating factor to see others and know your journey is close to being completed, but at the same time you also realize this magnificent trip will soon end.

A mile further (at 15.5 miles), you'll spot Mystery Falls, a 100-foot cascade sliding down the varnish covered canyon wall on the left (east).

Before you know it, you'll see gads of tourists loitering around and gawking upstream as you leave the river and hike the last mile along the paved sidewalk, finally reaching the Temple of Sinawava parking area, just over 17 miles from Chamberlain's Ranch. Take time to relax and reflect on one of the best (and most beautiful) hikes you'll ever experience.

≈ Trail Options:
Day hikers from Temple of Sinawava parking lot are advised to travel no further north than Big Springs (11 miles round-trip).

≈ Mileage Log from Chamberlain's Ranch Trailhead:
✿**Bulloch's Cabin:** 3 miles
✿**First narrows:** 6 miles
✿**Twelve foot waterfall:** 7 miles
✿**Deep Creek confluence:** 7.5 miles
✿**Kolob Creek confluence:** 10.5 miles
✿**Goose Creek confluence:** 11.5 miles
✿**Big Springs:** 12.25 miles
✿**Orderville Canyon confluence:** 14.5 miles
✿**Mystery Falls:** 15.5 miles
✿**Riverside Walk (pavement):** 16 miles
✿**Temple of Sinawava parking area:** 17 miles

≈ Other Area Trails and Attractions:

✿**West Rim Trail to Angels Landing:** This moderate to strenuous hike is second only to the Narrows for its breathtaking scenery and spectacular views down into Zion Canyon. It's not for the faint-hearted; my guess is that less than half of those taking this trail make it up to the narrow ridge of Angel's Landing.

✿**Observation Point:** Scenic and well-traveled, this trail takes you to one of the best view points in the park.

✿**Taylor Creek Trail, Kolob Canyons:** A delightful hike along the Middle Fork of Taylor Creek past a couple of historic cabins and ending at beautiful Double Arch Alcove

✿**Bryce Canyon National Park:** Another great hiking park just up the road. See the Navajo–Peekaboo–Queen's Garden Loop hike described on page 94.

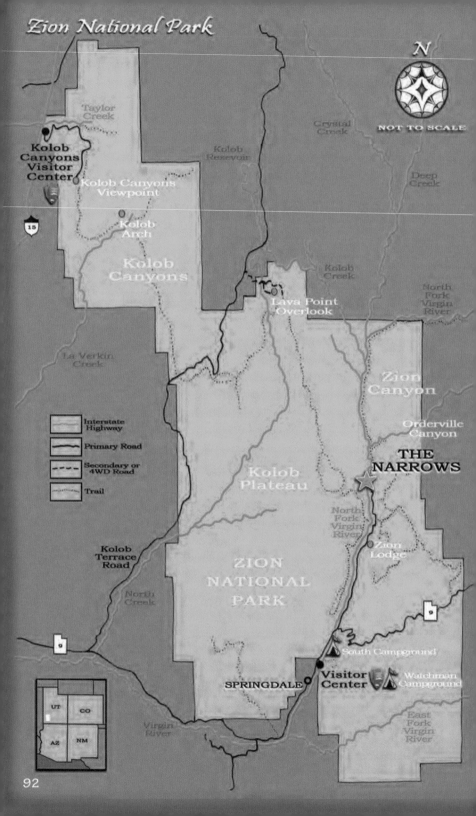

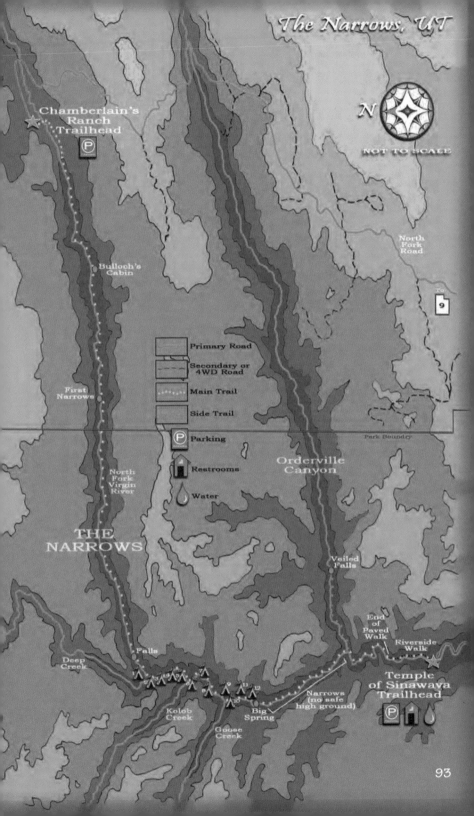

Navajo–Peekaboo–
Queen's Garden Loop

Bryce Canyon National Park
Utah

≋ Claim to Fame:

Bryce Canyon is a unique land of mysterious hoodoos and forests of stone colored a brilliant orange-red. The name is a misnomer, since this is not really a canyon but an amphitheater replete with a fantasyland of incredible rock formations. Dropping 2,000 feet in elevation from rim to base, the park harbors three distinct ecosystems, including Pinyon-Juniper, Ponderosa Pine, and Spruce-Fir habitats. It is the unique geological features however, that prompted Bryce Canyon's designation as a national park.

The Navajo–Peekaboo–Queen's Garden Loop captures the essence of this park, and provides one of the best day-hiking explorations of this sublime region, all in less than 6.5 miles of foot travel. Combining three classic trails into one larger figure-eight loop indulges hikers hoping to witness some of the best scenery Bryce Canyon offers. Descending into the amphitheater, these paths are moderate to somewhat strenuous (climbing out). Anyone who loves the outdoors should take time, or make time, to enjoy this resplendently hued and surreal excursion through the heart of one of the most geologically astonishing parks in the world.

≋ Park Overview:
✿**Closest town:** Bryce Canyon City (2.5 miles)
✿**Park elevations:** 6,620–9,115 feet
✿**Park established:** September 15, 1928
✿**Area:** 35,835 acres
✿**Annual visitation:** 1,285,492

≋ Getting There:
✿**Airport:**
♦McCarran Airport, Las Vegas, NV (270 miles)
♦Salt Lake City Airport, Salt Lake City, UT (270 miles)

✿**Vehicle:**
♦From US 89 take State Route 12 east 13 miles, and turn south (right) on SR 63 and travel another 4.5 miles to the entry station.

♦If driving from the west, follow State Route 12, passing the town of Tropic and staying on SR 12 for about 6.5 miles more. Then head south (left) on SR 63 another 4.5 miles to the entry station.

≋ Contact:
✿**Web:** www.nps.gov/brca
✿**Phone:** (435) 834-5322
✿**Mail:** Bryce Canyon NP, P.O. Box 640201, Bryce Canyon, UT 84764

≈ The Layout:

Bryce Canyon is one of the smallest national parks in the southwest, but due to its close proximity to other popular parks and its spectacular scenery, this geological gem receives quite a lot of visitation. With an average elevation over 8,000 feet along the rim, it is also quite a bit cooler than other area parks, with summer days averaging in the 80s, and nighttime lows dipping into the 40s. Hiking season at Bryce is late spring through early fall, although snowshoeing in winter, when the trails are cold and quiet, is great fun. Pets must be leashed at all times and are permitted only on paved roads, in campgrounds, parking lots, and viewpoints, but not in buildings or on unpaved surfaces. You are required to pick up after your pets.

Lodging can be found inside the park at the historic Bryce Canyon Lodge (reservations are a must), or outside the park entrance along the SR 63. Camping is available inside and outside the park. Most other amenities, (camping, gas, food, lodging, and car care), are available prior to entering the park along SR 63 in Bryce Canyon City. Additional lodging can be found to the east on SR 12 in Panguitch and Tropic.

SR 63, or as many call it, the Rim Road, serves as the main drive for all scenic overlooks and trailheads within the park. Otherwise, a few short side roads off the Rim Road provide access to specific scenic points and trailheads. Please note that trailers are not allowed on SR 63 past Sunset Campground. The Rim Road is 18 miles in length and stays to the west side of the canyon. Nearly all hiking trails drop steeply off the rim to the east of the Rim Road, offering access down into the color-filled amphitheater. Viewing the various geological wonders of vivid orange-red is what draws well over a million people to visit this national park each year.

≈ Permits and Restrictions:

Open year round, 24 hours a day, $25 fee per vehicle, or $12 per individual (motorcycle, bicycle, walk-in). No permits are required for day hikes, but if you are planning to stay overnight in the backcountry, a permit is required and can be purchased at the visitor center for $5–15, depending on the size of the group.

≈ Trail Overview:

This trail description is from Sunset Point Trailhead to Sunrise Point Trailhead. This trail is done as a day hike.

⚙ **Length:** 6.5 miles
⚙ **Difficulty:** Moderate to Strenuous
⚙ **Elevations:** 7,390–8,002 feet
⚙ **Hiking times:** 4–5 hours
⚙ **Water availability:** Water can be found at the campgrounds, and bottled water is available for purchase at the general store. Drinking water

is also available seasonally at Sunset Point parking area. There is no reliable water source along this trail.

⚬**Toilets:** Toilets are available at Sunset Point and seasonally on Peekaboo Loop.

⚬**Special advisories:** Carry plenty of water for this hike. Water sources below the rim are not reliable, are turned off seasonally, and most are located far from this route. The sandstone walls and formations at Bryce are loose gravel, making them exceptionally dangerous to climb, and it is illegal within the park to scramble, climb, or slide along its slopes. Lightning poses a year-round danger but is especially prevalent late-June through September. Pets are not allowed on trails. During the warm season you'll be sharing the Peekaboo Trail with horses; when they approach, step off to the inside of the trail until they have passed. Do not attempt to touch or pet the horses as they pass.

⁓ Trailhead Directions:

The described route begins at Sunset Point. From the visitor center, head straight (south) on the Rim Road (SR 63) about 1.25 miles, turning left (east) toward Sunset Point. You'll reach the parking area 1.5 miles from the visitor center.

⁓ Trail Description:

This circuit combines three trails, part of Navajo Loop, Peekaboo Loop, and Queen's Garden, into one figure-eight loop. These trails are all well maintained and well signed. The Sunset Point Trailhead is located at the far right (south-southeast) end of the parking lot. The trail heads east, descending from the rim and quickly reaching a junction, where you will take the Navajo Loop Trail signed "Wall Street" (on right). A series of steep switchbacks soon takes you downcanyon and into the narrow confines of Wall Street, named for those tight Manhattan streets squeezed between soaring skyscrapers.

Thor's Hammer

A twisted pine along Peekaboo Loop

At 0.75 miles, you reach the first main junction, a four-way intersection (partially hidden by a rock outcropping) with Navajo Loop heading back up to Sunset Point (and therefore out of the canyon), Queen's Garden straight ahead, and Peekaboo Loop to the right. For this hike, take the trail that immediately hairpins to the right (south-south-east) to a short connector trail for Peekaboo Loop. After hiking about 1 mile total (0.25 miles from the junction) you reach the next intersection, where you'll want to head right (south) toward the Peekaboo Loop. In about 50 yards you reach the official beginning of Peekaboo. I suggest you head left (southeast), to hike this loop in a clockwise direction for a better view of the Wall of Windows.

Head uphill immediately and then back down the other side, an up-and-down rhythm you'll soon get used to. You'll see the Fairy Castle above to your left (east), with Bryce Point to the south-southeast. At 2.5 miles from the trailhead, you'll see the trail coming down from Bryce Point on the left (east). Stay to your right (south-southwest) to remain on Peekaboo Loop. Past the Bryce Point Trail junction, you'll head back downhill, soon encountering a horse corral and water trough. (Do not drink this water without treating it.) Less than 100 feet past the corral, you will see a spur path on the left (southeast) to the trail restroom (open seasonally, no water). Staying on the main trail, you'll begin to slowly curve back toward the north-northwest as the Wall of Windows comes into closer view off to your left (west). A tunnel cut through the trail wall allows passage as the trail winds around through stacks of hoodoos, soon passing the Cathedral (on your right) and other unique stone formations as you return to the loop trail junction, about 4 miles from the trailhead.

At this familiar junction, head left (north), then left again (west), back onto the connector trail. About 4.25 miles into your journey, you return to the Navajo Loop junction and take the right (northeast) fork, following the sign to Queen's Garden. This connector trail is relatively open as it meanders through the forest for about a mile until arriving at Queen's Garden, 5 miles from the trailhead. Here you'll see a spur trail on the left (west). Take this left for a nice view of the formation named after Queen Victoria, where this spur trail ends.

From Queens' Garden, head back to the last junction and follow the signs for the climb up to Sunrise Point. Upon reaching Sunrise Point, at 6 miles, you'll need to head left (south) along the rim for another half-mile, returning to your vehicle parked at Sunset Point—a mere 6.5 miles from the beginning of this glorious journey.

≈ Trail Options:

There are lots of options for hiking this area, depending on your time and stamina. You can do just Navajo Loop, or just Queen's Garden. You can access Peekaboo Loop from Bryce Point. If you wanted to do more, you could start (or end) with the Rim Trail off Sunset Point and eventually access Peekaboo Loop via Bryce Point Trail. So choose whichever combination most appeals to you, and enjoy this stunning natural wonderland.

≈ Mileage Log from the Trailhead:
○**Junction with Peekaboo connector:** 0.75 miles
○**Peekaboo Loop Trail:** Just over 1 mile
○**Bryce Point/Peekaboo junction:** 2.5 miles
○**End of Peekaboo:** 4 miles
○**Return to Navajo/Peekaboo/Queen's Garden junction:** 4.25 miles
○**Spur trail to Queen Victoria:** 5 miles
○**Sunrise Point:** 6 miles
○**Return to Sunset Point parking area:** 6.5 miles

≈ Other Area Trails and Attractions:

○**Fairyland Loop Trail:** This is another fantastic hiking loop at Bryce with more hoodoos and exquisite scenery, plus a spur trail to Tower Bridge, an orange limestone fin connecting two large pinnacles.

○**Red Canyon:** For a quiet hiking experience in another marvelous geological setting, go 12 miles west of Bryce Canyon. Although often touted as the less dramatic gateway to Bryce Canyon, Red Canyon is magnificent in its own right, with a half-dozen trails to explore.

○**Grand Staircase—Escalante National Monument and Zion National Park:** These two parks offer gorgeous places to explore just around the corner from Bryce Canyon.

Bryce Canyon National Park

To Panguitch

12

63

BRYCE CANYON CITY

12

To Tropic

Fairyland Point

Visitor Center

North Campground
Sunrise Point

NAVAJO - PEEKABOO - QUEEN'S GARDEN LOOP

Sunset Point

Sunset Campground

Inspiration Point

Paria View

Bryce Point

Swamp Canyon

BRYCE CANYON NATIONAL PARK

Tropic Resevoir

Dixie National Forest

——	Primary Road
- - -	Secondary or 4WD Road
·······	Trail

Farview Point

Natural Arch

Dixie National Forest

East Fork Sevier River

N

NOT TO SCALE

63

Rainbow Point

UT CO

AZ NM

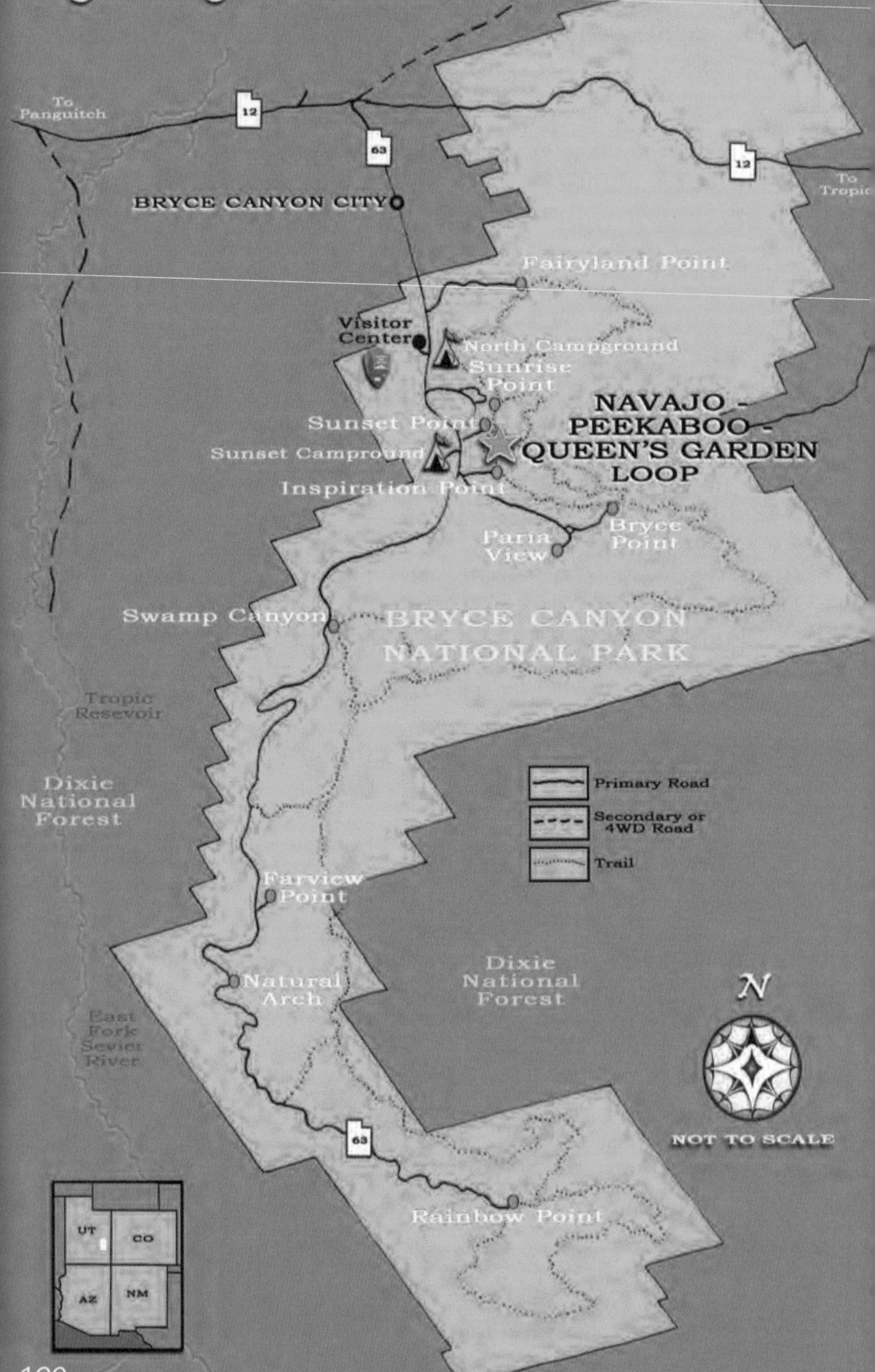

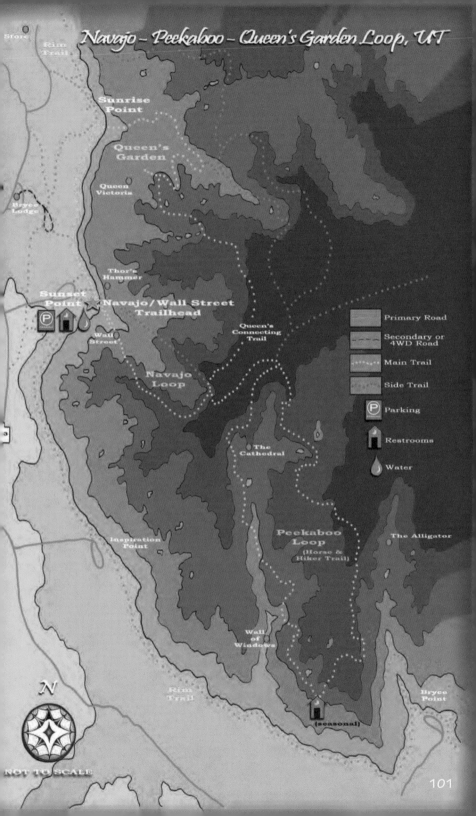

Navajo – Peekaboo – Queen's Garden Loop, UT

Store

Rim Trail

Sunrise Point

Queen's Garden

Queen Victoria

Bryce Lodge

Thor's Hammer

Sunset Point

Navajo/Wall Street Trailhead

Wall Street

Navajo Loop

Queen's Connecting Trail

The Cathedral

Inspiration Point

Peekaboo Loop
(Horse & Hiker Trail)

The Alligator

Wall of Windows

Rim Trail

Bryce Point

(seasonal)

Primary Road

Secondary or 4WD Road

Main Trail

Side Trail

P Parking

Restrooms

Water

N

NOT TO SCALE

Upper Muley Twist Canyon

Capitol Reef National Park

Utah

⩘ Claim to Fame:

Capitol Reef is a long, narrow park comprising over 375 square miles, and following a convoluted 100-mile wrinkle in Earth's crust known as the Waterpocket Fold. This park, once referred to as "Wayne Wonderland" (as in Wayne County, Utah), encompasses multicolored ridges and buttes, serpentine canyons, arches, spires, and numerous monoliths. The park was founded to protect its main geologic feature, the Waterpocket Fold, along with a bit of the region's natural color and cultural history.

While most tourists tend to visit the park's center at Fruita and take the Scenic Drive, the trail we'll be taking is in the southeast corner of the park along the fold. Upper Muley Twist Canyon features exciting vistas, soaring walls of striated and pockmarked rock, large tracts of open slickrock, numerous arches, and an enchanting narrow canyon. This trail and its sister trail, Lower Muley Twist, gained their collective name when it became clear that these canyons were so narrow they would "twist a mule." This is an exquisite hike filled with unique crimson cliffs, long views, and astounding rock wonders.

⩘ Park Overview:
⚙ **Closest town:** Torrey, UT (11 miles to the visitor center.)
⚙ **Park elevations:** 6,000–9,000 feet
⚙ **Park established:** December 18, 1971
⚙ **Area:** 241,904 acres
⚙ **Annual visitation:** 617,208

⩘ Getting There:
⚙ **Airport:**
♦ Grand Junction Regional Airport, Grand Junction, CO (220 miles)
♦ Salt Lake City Airport, Salt Lake City, UT (220 miles)
♦ McCarran Airport, Las Vegas, NV (340 miles)

⚙ **Vehicle:**
♦ From I-70 westbound, take Exit 149 to State Route 24 toward Hanksville. Proceed about 95 miles to the Capitol Reef Visitor Center.

♦ From I-70 eastbound, take the Exit 48 to State Route 24 toward Sigurd. Continue about 83 miles to the Capitol Reef Visitor Center.

♦ From Bryce Canyon, or Escalante, take State Route 12 eastbound. About 39 miles north of Boulder, just prior to entering the town of Torrey, take a right (east) onto SR 24 and proceed 11 miles to the Capitol Reef Visitor Center.

≈ Contact:
- ☼ **Web:** www.nps.gov/care
- ☼ **Phone:** (435) 425-3791
- ☼ **Mail:** Capitol Reef National Park, HC 70 Box 15, Torrey, UT 84775

≈ The Layout:
The park's most popular area is around the Fruita Historic District and Scenic Drive in the upper half of the park, but some of the best views and most varied hiking opportunities are along the lower area of the Waterpocket Fold in Strike Valley. At a slightly higher elevation, Capitol Reef is just a bit cooler than other area parks, but summer temperatures can still reach the 100-degree range, while nights are cool, in the 50s and 60s with low humidity. Most hiking is done during the spring and fall, or at the beginning or end of summer when the heat is less extreme. There are no amenities or lodging inside the park. Lodging choices are slim at Cainville and Hanksville to the east of the park, but there are several choices in the small town of Torrey to the west.

≈ Permits and Restrictions:
A $5 entrance fee is charged per vehicle (including motorcycles) for those traveling south beyond the Fruita Campground along the park's

View of the enormous Saddle Arch formation. The small pockmarks in the surrounding rocks are called "solution pockets." They form as water erodes weakly cemented portions of the sandstone.

John Ducasse heads into
Upper Muley Twist Canyon.

Scenic Drive. The fee for individuals (bicycles and pedestrians) is $3. Backcountry permits are required for overnight backpacking. Permits are free and can be obtained at the visitor center.

∿ Trail Overview:

This trail can be done as a long day hike or as an overnight backpack trip.

☼**Length:** 15 miles round-trip from 2WD parking area, or 9.5 miles from the 4WD parking, along a semi-looped trail.

☼**Difficulty:** Moderate to strenuous

☼**Elevations:** 5,730–6,690 feet

☼**Day-hike destinations:** Strike Valley Overlook, Saddle Arch

☼**Hiking times:** 5–8 hours

☼**Water availability:** This is a dry trail. Other than scarce rainwater, no water is available along the route.

☼**Toilets:** None

☼**Special advisories:** Extreme summer heat is always dangerous, and water sources are not reliable. This is normally a dry trail; always carry extra water supplies. Flash floods are a potential problem when hiking in any narrow slot canyons, especially during monsoon season, late June through September. Make sure you know the weather forecast before entering the canyon. The Rim Route is not recommended for small children or people with a fear of heights. When camping overnight, you are required to camp a minimum of a half-mile from all roads and trailheads. The upper (north) section of the canyon route can be an absolute bear for anyone with a full pack; therefore, it is recommended that you make camp and day hike most of the trail. The best campsites are prior to Saddle Arch and the southern section of the Rim Route just above the canyon. No pets are allowed in the backcountry, and they cannot be left unattended. Gathering wood and building campfires is strictly prohibited. Bicycles are not permitted on trails.

∿ Trailhead Directions:

From the visitor center, travel east 9 miles (temporarily leaving the park) and take Notom-Bullfrog Road right (south). Make sure you check the road conditions at the visitor center prior to heading into the backcountry since the Notom-Bullfrog Road can be impassable when wet.

At 5 miles the pavement ends, turning to a mostly gravel and clay surface, with occasional sandy areas. Continue south, keeping the green-gray plateau of Swap Mesa on your left (east) and the multicolored Waterpocket Fold on your right (west). After driving on the unpaved road for about 30 miles, you'll see a triangular junction (signed) where the road forks. Here you'll want to turn right (west) onto Burr Trail Road and proceed in a south-southwest direction as the road enters a box canyon. The road climbs the fold in a series of switchbacks and then levels out for a time. Continue about two miles on Burr Trail Road and take a right at the signed Strike Valley Overlook Road. The "strike" is a geological term referring to a tilted surface that has shifted horizontally along a fault. Passenger cars can usually proceed about a half-mile to a small parking area and trail register. Those with a high-clearance 4WD vehicle can continue another 3 miles to the end of the road. It can take about two hours traveling from the visitor center to the trailhead, if the road conditions are in your favor.

You can also reach the trailhead from SR 12 in Boulder, Utah, via the mostly paved and scenic Burr Trail Road. From Boulder, take Burr Trail Road east. You will pass through a magnificent red rock canyon en route, and in 30.5 miles you enter the park. At 33 miles turn left (northeast) to Strike Valley Overlook Road and the trailheads.

≈ Trail Description:

If you are beginning at the 2WD parking area and its trailhead, the road is the trail. The road will drop off into a wide sandy wash that moves east and quickly turns to the north-northwest. In about 1.75 miles you'll see Double Arch on the left (west), and at 3 miles you will reach the 4WD parking lot.

From the 4WD lot, you'll see a trail on the right (east) that ascends in a general northeast direction to the Strike Valley Overlook. (Make this side trip now or later, if you choose.) For Muley Twist Canyon continue following the wash, staying to the right on those occasions when the wash appears to fork, so as to remain in the main channel. This is a nice leisurely hike along a gravelly streambed with a few narrow rock channels to scramble through. Be careful walking the rock-strewn wash, or your hike could change from Muley Twist Canyon to "ankle twist canyon."

At about 1.5 miles, you can spot Muley Arch about 200 feet up to your left (west). Less than a quarter-mile further, you'll see Saddle Arch, again to your left. Across from the arch on the right (east), you'll see a small sign and cairns indicating the Rim Route, a total of 1.8 miles from the 4WD trailhead. To hike the loop in the somewhat easier clockwise direction, continue north along the rocky wash. (Taking the right would head up to the Rim Route section of the trail; we will exit the canyon this way instead.)

After passing the Rim Route and continuing up the wash, take the short detour up and around the canyon bottom; it soon returns to the wash. At 3.1 miles, you'll see three more arches, high off to the left (west). At 3.9 miles an unnamed double arch is visible in the same general direction but at the bottom of a slot canyon. Stay right (east) at the next wash junction, and soon the canyon trail tightens dramatically as it approaches the Pouroff. To go around this obstacle, you'll need to follow the rock cairns along the canyon's east wall (right) and ascend a shelf that climbs nearly 100 feet up from the streambed. This section would be tough with a full pack, due to the narrow trail and obstructing vegetation. Stay above the narrow streambed until you reach 4.5 miles, when the path drops back to the bottom of the wash. An old uranium mine exists near the Pouroff along the wash. Avoid it if you happen to be traveling along the bottom of the canyon (which normally you wouldn't).

By the time you've hit the 4.8 mile mark, you'll spot a sign down in the wash announcing the Rim Route section. From here, you depart the canyon. You do not want to lose the trail here, so be even more attentive watching for the plentiful stone cairns. If you travel more than

The Rim Route looking west

about 100 feet without seeing a rock stack, you've probably wandered off trail, so backtrack to the last cairn before continuing.

Continue your ascent, scrambling almost straight up (in some cases hand-over-hand climbing) along the canyon's east wall. Soon the trail will double back a bit and head through a break in the sandstone cliff. Before you know it, you'll find yourself up on the crest of the Waterpocket Fold. (You'll probably spot a sign off to the left announcing the trail down to the Canyon Route, which you just climbed.) The long views here are exquisite and continue for the next two miles as you head south-southeast on top of the world. To the right (west), you'll be looking down at the canyon of red-colored Wingate sandstone you just hiked through, with Grand Gulch, Swap, and Tarantula Mesa seen farther off to the left (east). Some sections along this part of the trail are along exposed and precarious slickrock ledges where extreme caution is required, especially if you are carrying a backpack, or when it's icy or wet. Don't presume you know where the route goes —be attentive and closely follow the rock stacks.

Nearing 7.3 miles, be alert for the small sign that directs you back down to the Canyon Route. Closely follow the cairns again as the trail descends in a northwest pattern, crossing slickrock ledges, dropping down in loose rock, and descending back into Muley Twist Canyon near Saddle Arch at 7.6 miles. This area should appear familiar as you take the left (south) and follow the wash the remaining 1.8 miles, retracing the trail back to the 4WD parking area. (If you parked here, your hike would total 9.5 miles.) After returning to the 4WD parking area, consider heading up the trail to Strike Valley Overlook, although if you've hiked the Rim Route on Muley, you will have already enjoyed a similar view. This half-mile round trip is well worth the minimal effort to climb up for another awesome view. If you parked at the 2WD trailhead, you'll backtrack another 3 miles along the road to reach your vehicle.

≈ Trail Options:

From the 2WD parking area you can day-hike up to Strike Valley Overlook and along Upper Muley to Saddle Arch for a nearly ten-mile round-trip jaunt. You could also day hike from the 4WD trailhead to Saddle Arch, 3.5 miles round-trip, for a nice easy stroll.

≈ Mileage Log from the Trailhead:

✧**Upper Muley Twist Canyon Trailhead (2WD parking) to 4WD parking and Strike Valley Overlook Trailhead:** 3 miles
✧**4WD parking area to Strike Valley Overlook:** 0.25 miles
✧**4WD parking area to Saddle Arch:** 1.8 miles
✧**4WD parking area to Pouroff:** 4.2 miles
✧**4WD parking area to Rim Route:** 4.8 miles
✧**Return to Canyon Route:** 7.7 miles
✧**Return to trailhead:** Total 15.5 miles round-trip from 2WD parking area, or 9.5 miles from the 4WD parking

≈ Other Area Trails and Attractions:

✧**Lower Muley Twist Canyon:** Lower Muley is the natural downstream extension of the Upper Muley, with the canyon divided by Burr Trail Road. It contains a few nice alcoves, some narrow slots, and overall is a very pleasant hike.

✧**Grand Gulch/Cassidy Arch:** Combining these two trails provides many of the scenic highlights known to Capitol Reef, impressive narrows amidst sandstone canyons, plus a climb to Cassidy Arch with its sheer cliffs and superb views.

✧**Hickman Bridge Trail:** The park's most popular hike contains a variety of natural scenery and its namesake, a beautiful natural stone bridge towering 125 feet above the easy trail.

✧**Canyonlands National Park, The Maze:** The Maze is the most inaccessible region of Canyonlands National Park, but the area includes some awesome canyons. Getting to most trailheads requires hours of driving along unimproved roads. In particular, Horseshoe Canyon offers a gorgeous canyon with a significant rock art collection.

✧**Natural Bridges National Monument:** Containing three huge natural bridges, this park has been a national monument since 1908. There are many hikes to choose from and they are all delightful.

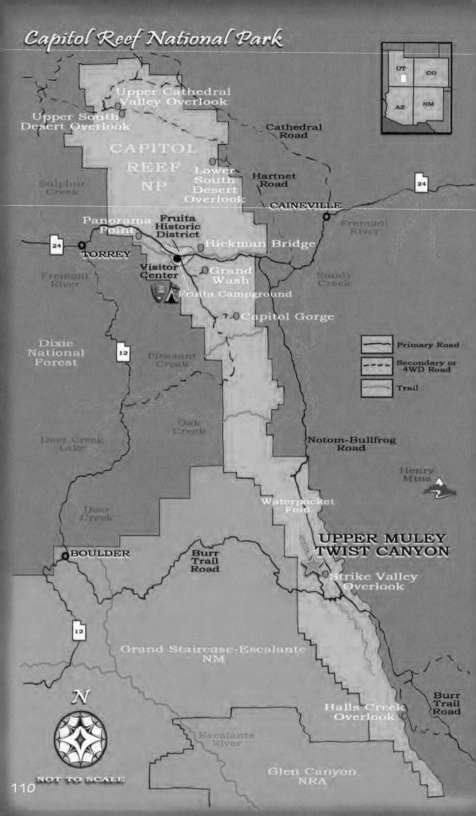

Capitol Reef National Park

Upper Cathedral Valley Overlook

Upper South Desert Overlook

CAPITOL REEF NP

Sulphur Creek

Cathedral Road

Lower South Desert Overlook

Hartnet Road

CAINEVILLE

Fremont River

24

Panorama Point

Fruita Historic District

Hickman Bridge

24

TORREY

Visitor Center

Grand Wash

Fremont River

Fruita Campground

Sandy Creek

Capitol Gorge

Dixie National Forest

12

Pleasant Creek

Oak Creek

Deer Creek Lake

Notom-Bullfrog Road

Henry Mtns

Deer Creek

Waterpocket Fold

BOULDER

Burr Trail Road

UPPER MULEY TWIST CANYON

Strike Valley Overlook

12

Grand Staircase-Escalante NM

Burr Trail Road

Halls Creek Overlook

N

Escalante River

Glen Canyon NRA

NOT TO SCALE

UT   CO
AZ   NM

Primary Road

Secondary or 4WD Road

Trail

110

Upper Muley Twist Canyon, UT

NOT TO SCALE

Waterpocket Fold

Trail Sign

The Pouroff

Trail Sign

Unnamed Double Arch

Notom - Bullfrog Road

Unnamed Arches

Strike Valley

Park Boundary

Saddle Arch

Trail Sign

Muley Arch

UPPER MULEY TWIST CANYON

Swap Mesa

4WD Trailhead

Strike Valley Overlook

Double Arch

Peekaboo Arch

Burr Trail Road

Picnic Area

2WD Trailhead

Surprise Canyon

LOWER MULEY TWIST CANYON

Headquarters Canyon

Primary Road

Secondary or 4WD Road

Main Trail

Side Trail

Parking

West Fork Oak Creek

Coconino National Forest

Arizona

≈ Claim to Fame:

Coconino National Forest, one of the most picturesque and diverse in the country, ranges from high desert to high alpine environments, red rocks to thick conifer woodlands. The forest rises to the north, surrounding the San Francisco Peaks, and to the south it drops precipitously off the Mogollon Plateau and into the red-orange colored, water-carved canyons in and around Sedona. This national forest is divided into three varied districts: the mountainous Flagstaff District, the Mogollon Rim District (the southern terminus of the Colorado Plateau), and the Red Rock District around Sedona. With over 150 trails to choose from, this region is not what most people think of when imagining the stark Arizona environment of sandy deserts littered with dry cow skulls, although in summer the scorching temperatures and lack of humidity will remind you often enough that you are still very much in the desert Southwest.

The West Fork of Oak Creek (within the boundaries of Red Rock–Secret Mountain Wilderness) is a spectacular riparian oasis where author Zane Grey is said to have penned his famous novel *Call of the Canyon*. This extraordinary ecosystem—towering cliffs amidst a mixed conifer-deciduous forest, with a charming creek running through it—makes for an enchanting hike. Unfortunately, if you are looking for solitude, you won't find it on this overwhelmingly popular trail (the most popular in Coconino National Forest), especially on weekends in the warm season and during fall color. But if you are looking for a cool, lush canyon to hike or stroll, this journey is undoubtedly the best creek-side hike in the Southwest. Despite the crowds, it is simply serene.

≈ Area Overview:
✧**Closest towns:** Sedona, AZ (9.5 miles), Flagstaff, AZ (17.5 miles)
✧**Coconino National Forest elevations:** 2,600–12,637 feet
✧**National Forest established:** July 2, 1908
✧**Area:** 1,821,495 acres
✧**Annual visitation:** 1,890,000

≈ Getting There:
✧**Airport:**
♦Sky Harbor Airport, Phoenix, AZ (145 miles)
♦McCarran Airport, Las Vegas, NV (345 miles)

✧**Vehicle:**
♦From Flagstaff, take I-17 south for two miles. Take Exit 337 and turn right, then make a quick left (south) onto US 89A. In about 15 miles, after coming down the switchbacks into Oak Creek Canyon, you'll see trailhead signs indicating Call of the Canyon day-use area on your right (west). Enter the parking area, where you will immediately see the fee station.

◆From US 89A in Sedona, head north into Oak Creek Canyon for 9.5 miles. You'll see trailhead signs to Call of the Canyon day-use area on your left (west). Enter the parking area, where you will immediately see the fee station.

∼ Contact:
○ **Web:** www.fs.usda.gov/coconino
○ **Phone:** Red Rock Ranger District (928) 203-7500
○ **Mail:** Red Rock Ranger District, P.O. Box 20429, Sedona, AZ 86341

∼ The Layout:
West Fork Trail is an easy trail to access since the path originates just off the highway in Oak Creek Canyon. Parking is fairly limited, and it is recommended that on most days and especially on busy weekends you get to the trailhead parking lot by at least 10 a.m. or you may have to look for parking along the highway. Also popular, Slide Rock State Park is located a few miles south of West Fork, and this area too can be quite congested during summer weekends and holidays. The closest amenities are in Sedona, a tourist town that accommodates a multitude of visitors with a variety of lodging and dining options. Most developed trails and attractions within the Red Rock Ranger District require the purchase of a Red Rock Pass for $5 (daily), $15 (weekly), or $20 (annual).

At an average 5,300 foot elevation and deeply shaded, West Fork can be hiked any time of year. It is gorgeous at all times but especially in fall, and October is the busiest month for visitation as the bigtooth maples and box elders come into autumn color. The trail can be undertaken as a 7-mile day hike (round trip) or a 14-mile overnight backpacking excursion (with shuttle vehicle). By getting your feet wet and plodding on, you can easily continue past the spot where the majority of visitors turn around, when the trail enters the water and the canyon narrows. Whichever way you plan this hike, the West Fork of Oak Creek leaves an indelible impression on all who enter its rich riparian habitat.

∼ Permits and Restrictions:
A user fee of $9 per vehicle (up to 5

A typical scene along West Fork Trail

people) is required for parking at Call of the Canyon day-use area. Walk-ins are $2 per person. The trail is open all year, but the booth is not staffed in the off-season, so make sure you have the correct change for the requisite fee. Operational hours are 9 a.m. - 8 p.m., except for winters, when hours are 9 a.m. to dusk. The gate is usually open by 8 a.m.

Red Rock Passes are not accepted here because the day-use area is managed by a concessionaire. "Big Three" annual passes are available from Recreation Resource Management (RRM) for access to day-use areas at Call of the Canyon day-use area, Grasshopper Point (swimming area), and Crescent Moon Ranch (Red Rock Crossing). Passes are available at each of the three day-use areas (when the booths are staffed), at the Oak Creek Visitor Center at Indian Gardens in Oak Creek Canyon (US 89A), or at the North Gateway Visitor Center at Oak Creek Vista Overlook (US 89A).

∾ Trail Overview:

This trail description is from Call of the Canyon day-use and parking area to the 4-mile day hike destination. Note: The official day hike mileage (one way) is 3.5 miles from the West Fork Oak Creek Trailhead, but this does not include the half-mile from the trailhead and kiosk to Call of the Canyon parking lot. This trail is usually done as a day hike, but some will backpack overnight after hiking a minimum of six miles into the canyon.

⟡**Length:** 8 miles round-trip (day hike), 14 miles total length (overnight through-hike)

⟡**Difficulty:** Easy–moderate (day hike) to moderate–strenuous (overnight)

⟡**Elevations:** 5,260–5,510 feet

⟡**Hiking times:** 4–5 hours

⟡**Water availability:** No drinking water is available at the trailhead. Creek water must be treated before consumption.

⟡**Toilets:** Composting toilets are available at the trailhead parking area.

⟡**Special advisories:** No overnight camping is allowed within 6 miles of the trailhead. Although considered an easy hike, West Fork does require frequent water crossings on slippery rocks and logs; caution is advised, and hiking sticks can prove helpful. Pets are allowed but must be leashed at all times. No campfires are allowed at any time throughout the full 14-mile length of the canyon. There is no maintained trail beyond the day-hike destination at about 4 miles from the parking area. Do not attempt this hike if storms are forecast. There is a high risk of flash floods along West Fork and Oak Creek, especially during monsoon season (mid-June through September).

≈ Trailhead Directions:

The trailhead is located at the parking area for Call of the Canyon Day-Use and Picnic Area in Oak Creek Canyon 9.5 miles north of Sedona, Arizona, via US 89A. The trailhead is located to the left (south) of the restrooms, next to the large stone kiosk introducing the Call of the Canyon day-use area and its trails.

≈ Trail Description:

The description covers the popular day-hike into the canyon. Those wanting to through-hike the full 14 miles of West Fork to Forest Road 231 must be prepared to wade and swim through several pools, hop over miles of boulders, and enjoy the solitude of a stunning wilderness. The through-hike can be done as a 2-day backpack to the rim, if you shuttle a vehicle, or as a 3–4 day excursion by retracing the same route.

From the trailhead, follow the path toward the creek, and in about 150 feet you'll pass along the steel bridge crossing over Oak Creek. After the bridge, the trail turns left (south) and crosses through a historic apple orchard before curving west-northwest, where you will find yourself in the midst of what is left of the old Mayhew Lodge. The remnants of this once famous inn can be seen here—a part of a wall, some chicken coops, and a smokehouse. The lodge burned down in 1980, leaving just a few tattered memories of its heyday when it hosted presidents, movie stars, and authors like Zane Grey.

The trail curves back to the south and, at nearly 0.5 miles from the parking lot, you'll see the official trailhead kiosk for the West Fork Oak Creek Trail, a sign-in register, and (usually) an array of tree-branch hiking staffs for those in need. Note the poison ivy along the sides of the trail just past the register: This weed to grows throughout the moist canyon, prompting the reminder "leaves of three—let it be."

At about 0.6 miles, you'll cross the creek (the first of about a dozen such crossings, although the number can vary depending on your chosen route). Note that nearly all official crossings are marked with 3- to 4-foot tall cairns made of wire baskets filled with red rock.

Take your time making these stream crossings: Wet logs and rocks are notoriously slick, so try finding dry ones. Use hiking sticks for balance, and test your steps onto logs and stones that might be unsteady before you commit. When all else fails, go ahead and simply walk in the creek. In the summer it feels great.

History tells us that the first "old world" explorers to visit any part of the American Southwest were three shipwrecked Spaniards, including Alvar Nuñez Cabeza de Vaca, who landed near what is now Galveston, Texas, in 1528. One member of this group, a North African man named Esteban, is said to have reached the Colorado Plateau in 1536. By some accounts, the Zuni people rescued him from slavery by claiming he was dead and subsequently allowing him to stay and raise a family within the tribal community.

The search for the Southwest's mythical cities of gold brought the Spanish onto the plateau throughout the late 1500s. Among them was Garcia Lopes de Cardenas, who became the first European to see the Grand Canyon in 1540. Failing to find golden riches put a kink in the plans of the Spanish, and for the next century the only Spaniards to venture into the region were Franciscan missionaries eager to spread Christianity to the indigenous peoples. With the introduction of European diseases, Native American tribes were decimated as epidemics of smallpox and measles swept through the region. During the seventeenth and eighteenth centuries, the Spanish continually fought with many of the native tribes who were conducting raids against their missions. The conflicts ultimately discouraged white settlement along most of the Colorado Plateau until the mid-1800s.

Traders helped establish some of the famous Southwest trail routes, including the Old Spanish Trail and the Mormon Trail, in the early 1800s. American explorers began to make their way onto the plateau by the middle of the century, and Mormon settlers were entering the Great Salt Lake Basin by 1848. The most famous explorer in the Southwest was John Wesley Powell, leader of the first expedition along the Green and Colorado Rivers, and through the Grand Canyon in 1869.

The last half of the nineteenth century saw the introduction of miners, ranchers, missionaries, loners, and outlaws to the area, all trying to scratch out a living from the harsh environment. Nowadays, visitors in and around the plateau's numerous parks and monuments provide a major source of income for the region. Tourism joins mining, ranching, and the ever-present construction industry, as the principal economic drivers.

The Subway—to continue from here you must get your feet wet.
This is the turnaround point for most folks.

After the third stream crossing, or about 1 mile, you'll come to an area of open slickrock where the creek flows through a narrow slit in the streambed. This area is extremely popular for swimming, and on warm weekends you'll see lots of families playing here in the creek. Looking off to the right, you'll spot a rock-cage cairn set there to keep folks on the trail. Stay to the right, following the cairns, as the trail steps back up onto the creek's bank and continues on through the forest.

In early summer you'll see large areas of purple lupines blooming along the trail and forests of ferns amidst the maples, oaks, and fir trees. The trail meanders back and forth across the stream, well worn and easy to follow. Just past the seventh crossing, at about 1.8 miles, you should spot a 5-foot-tall brown trail maker just up the embankment from the creek. At nearly 2 miles from the parking lot, you'll pass next to a huge slanted boulder that was dislodged in the late 1990s, altering the trail as it slammed into the soft sand below. Mushroom Rock, one of the nicest picnic spots along the trail, is at 2.6 miles where the stream has undercut the sandstone, forming a half-mushroom shape. It's a great place to sit; drape your legs over the edge and relax a bit.

After the tenth crossing, about 2.8 miles from the trailhead, you should see an alcove off to the left that makes another nice place to picnic, but remember: There is no camping allowed here. Just after the twelfth creek crossing, at about 3.5 miles, you'll climb up along the rocks and ascend a stone stairway, taking you to an area of the trail that stays well above the creek before the trail eventually drops back down to the creekbed.

The official day-hike trail ends just shy of 4 miles from the parking area. Here the creek enters a narrow subway-like section, and most people turn around. You can go on if you want, but from late fall through winter and spring, the water is often too cold to continue without special gear and can be waist deep through this narrow section. If you decide to continue, however, you should know that this hike only gets more fun as the masses are left behind, your feet are wet, and you can enjoy some amazing sections of wilderness that the others who have already turned around will have missed. Before too long, you'll encounter a canyon pool that is just too deep to walk through, and you'll have to swim to go any further. This is another popular turn-around point, and it makes for a nice full day hike.

After reaching the destination of your choosing, return via the same trail, backtracking to the Call of the Canyon parking area. The round-trip mileage is nearly 8 total miles from the parking lot trailhead to the narrows and back. You've now experienced one of the most magical riparian canyons in the world. Feels good doesn't it?

⁓ Trail Options:
Overnight trips can extend another 10 miles to the end of the canyon at Forest Road 231, but backpackers must travel a minimum of 6 miles from the trailhead before making camp.

⁓ Mileage Log from Call of the Canyon Parking Area:
✪**West Fork Oak Creek Trailhead:** 0.5 miles
✪**First creek crossing:** 0.6 miles
✪**Boulder fall:** 2 miles
✪**Mushroom Rock:** 2.6 miles
✪**End of official day-hike trail:** 4 miles (from parking area)

⁓ Other area trails and attractions:

✪**Bear Mountain:** A strenuous hike in Sedona that climbs above Fay Canyon to provide one of the best scenic vistas in an area known for scenic vistas

✪**Sycamore Canyon Wilderness:** Like West Fork, this is another gorgeous riparian hike along a relatively unknown wild creekside trail. Sycamore Canyon Wilderness, designated in 1935, was one the first wilderness areas protected in Arizona.

✪**West Clear Creek:** A nearly forty-mile trek along a riparian corridor that is considered one of the most scenic, yet least visited regions in Arizona

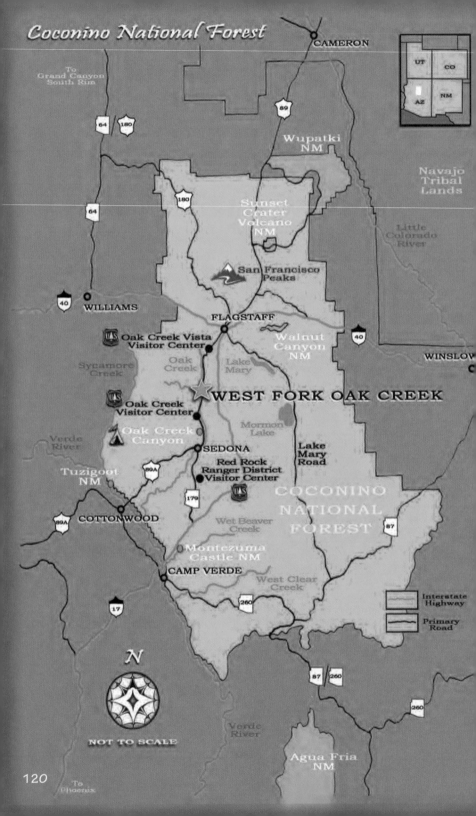

West Fork Oak Creek, AZ

To Flagstaff

89A

Oak Creek Vista
Visitor Center

West Fork
Oak Creek

To
Forest Road
231

6 Miles:
(camping is allowed
beyond this point)

Pine
Flat
Campground

WEST FORK
OAK CREEK

Harding
Point

Oak
Creek

	Primary Road
	Secondary or 4WD Road
	Main Trail
	Side Trail
P	Parking
	Restrooms

End
of Trail

Cave
Spring
Campground

Call
of the
Canyon
Day Use
Area
(West Fork
Trailhead)

P

Barney
Pasture

Lookout
Tower

Bootlegger
Campground

N

Red Rock
Secret Mountain
Wilderness

89A

NOT TO SCALE

To
Sedona

121

White House Ruins

Canyon de Chelly National Monument

Arizona

⚞ Claim to Fame:

Canyon de Chelly is one of the longest continuously inhabited areas in North America. Calling the monument Canyon de Chelly is a bit of a misnomer since there are two separate canyons, Canyon del Muerto to the north and Canyon de Chelly to the south; both empty into Chinle Wash. The monument consists of a rim of sandstone overlooking a beautifully majestic canyon, with an intermittent creek weaving its way amid green-hued banks and numerous ancient ruins. Relatively unknown, this sinuous, buff-red sandstone canyon may not be quite as spectacular as some of the deeper chasms in Arizona, but it provides a more intimate feel, making visitors give pause and perhaps seek more insight into the lives of its inhabitants. The monument encompasses several scenic overlooks, one wonderful hike (more if you hire a guide), and the magnificent, 800-foot twin towers of Spider Rock.

Like Navajo National Monument, Canyon de Chelly is owned by the Navajo Nation but administered by the National Park Service. Although White House Ruin Trail is the only trail unsupervised hikers can do without a Navajo guide, it is a delightful exploration back in time. I must admit that I've included this hike as "one of the best canyon hikes in the southwest" more for the purpose of drawing visitors to this resplendent national monument, and to experience the whole of the canyon, than merely for the hike itself. That said, this trail is still one of the most delightful and geologically and culturally intriguing hikes listed in this book. Though this is a relatively small canyon, the red-pigmented rocks and sheer sandstone walls rising up 1,000 feet from the canyon floor are dramatic and strikingly beautiful. Few would ever deny Canyon de Chelly its place among the most beautiful canyons the American Southwest has to offer.

⚞ Park Overview:
- ✧**Closest town:** Chinle, AZ (3 miles)
- ✧**Park elevations:** 5,500–7,000 feet
- ✧**Park established:** April 1, 1931
- ✧**Area:** 83,840 acres
- ✧**Annual visitation:** 827,247

⚞ Getting There:
✧**Airport:**
- ♦Sky Harbor Airport, Phoenix, AZ (353 miles)
- ♦Albuquerque Airport, Albuquerque, NM (245 miles)

✧**Vehicle:**
- ♦From State Route 191 in Chinle, Arizona head east on Indian Route 7 about three miles to the visitor center on the right.

⏤ Contact:
☼**Web:** www.nps.gov/cach
☼**Phone:** (928) 674-5500
☼**Mail:** Canyon de Chelly NM, P.O. Box 588, Chinle, AZ 86503

⏤ The Layout:
Canyon de Chelly is home to several Navajo families; therefore, most areas are restricted without a native guide. Most canyon inhabitants live along the rim during winter months and return to their inner canyon homes during the warm season. The best time of the year to visit is from mid-spring to mid-fall; summers bring the usual high-desert heat and dryness. Expect summer temperatures to be in the 90-100 degree range, with lows around 50 degrees. Canyon colors can be spectacular during the fall, when cottonwoods turn gold. The most popular attractions are the South Rim Drive and Spider Rock Overlook. Services and amenities are located in the town of Chinle, though Thunderbird Lodge has a cafeteria and gift shop. Hiring a native guide to explore the inner canyon is highly recommended for those who want an intimate sense of the canyon. Also, you should expect to find artists and craftspeople at nearly every popular stop in and around the canyon. These vendors are trying to make a living selling their wonderful wares; please take the time to browse and make a purchase if you find something that calls to you.

⏤ Permits and Restrictions:
This park is a non-fee area, although donations are greatly appreciated. There are no entry fees, but the Navajo Parks and Recreation Department operates Cottonwood Campground and does collect a fee for camping. Private hikes and tours within the depths of the canyon can be arranged, and reservations are recommended.

⏤ Trail Overview:
This trail is done as a day-hike.
☼**Length:** 2.5 miles
☼**Difficulty:** Easy to moderate
☼**Elevations:** 5,500–6,000 feet
☼**Hiking time:** 2 hours

✿**Water availability:** This is essentially a dry trail. (Chinle Wash may contain water, but it is not recommended for consumptive use and must be treated before drinking.)

✿**Toilets:** There are no toilets at the trailhead, but there are composting toilets across from the ruins inside the canyon.

✿**Special advisories:** After it leaves the paved sidewalk the trail is steep and the top is precipitous. Exercise caution if you are hiking with small children. No pets are allowed on the trail. Visitors are advised to be respectful toward the canyon's inhabitants. Please remain on the trail, and properly dispose of any personal litter. It is customary to request permission prior to photographing any local Navajos or their property, and a small fee should also be paid as a matter of courtesy.

〰 **Trailhead Directions:**
About 7 miles along the South Rim Drive, you'll see the sign to White House Ruins Overlook. Turn left (north-northwest) and proceed to the parking area. The trail splits off to the right along the sidewalk that heads toward the overlook.

Looking down into the canyon about one-quarter of the way into the trail

≈ Trail Description:

This trail is one of my favorite short hikes. Standing on the edge, looking down into the canyon, the hike may seem a bit precarious, but take heart—it is a very pleasant and well-worn trail. From the parking area, follow the sidewalk and signs to the White House Ruin Trail as it splits off to the right. The railing ends, and you continue on slickrock along the rim in a southerly direction, following arrows and footprints chiseled into the slickrock. Soon the trail curves sharply to the north, and you'll see a large sign warning visitors not to photograph the Navajo people (which caused three young Navajo girls in front of us to laugh that they weren't allowed to take pictures of each other).

The trail almost immediately begins its descent heading into the first of two tunnels. Descending steeply, with numerous switchbacks, the narrow trail hugs the canyon's sandstone walls amidst swirling and striated rock. There are plenty of nicely situated benches along the way to rest and contemplate the canyon. At about 1 mile, you'll pass through

View from the trail looking up at the canyon's rim and a wall of varnished De Chelly Formation sandstone

a second sandstone tunnel and realize that you are nearly at the canyon's bottom. Upon reaching the canyon floor, the hike turns into a comfortable amble over to the ruins. You'll pass through an area of burnt stumps, part of an aggressive program to remove invasive Russian olive and tamarisk trees from the canyon. You'll see a footbridge crossing the wash and, on the opposite side of the canyon you'll spot the ruins.

These ruins date back to the 1000s, built and occupied by the Ancestral Puebloans. The well-preserved masonry buildings lie beneath a 500-foot sheer vertical cliff. The upper and lower levels contain about sixty rooms and four kivas (larger rooms used as gathering places). The ruins were named for the white-plastered walls of the upper-most section. Take pictures, enjoy the architecture, experience a bit of the culture, and return along the same trail.

⚝ Trail Options:
There really are no other options for hiking this short trail. If you would like a more meaningful learning experience at Canyon de Chelly, please consider hiring a Navajo guide to allow yourself a more extensive exploration into what are otherwise off-limits areas of the canyons.

⚝ Mileage Log from the Trailhead:
✿**First tunnel:** .25 miles
✿**Second tunnel:** 1 mile
✿**Canyon floor:** 1.1 miles
✿**White House ruins:** 1.25 miles

⚝ Other Area Trails and Attractions:

✿**Hubbell Trading Post National Historic Site:** Take a journey back to the 1880s with a visit to this historic trading post, the oldest continuously operating trading post on the Navajo Nation.

✿**Monument Valley Navajo Tribal Park:** This iconic valley was used as the backdrop for many a Hollywood western movie. There is one unguided trail (the Wildcat Trail, a 3.2 mile loop around the West Mitten), and the drive through the valley is magnificent.

✿**Long Logs Trail, Petrified Forest National Park:** The 1.6-mile loop has one of the highest concentrations of petrified logs among the park's short trails. This park is world renowned not only for its huge collection of petrified trees but also for containing significant fossils from the Late Triassic Period.

Canyon De Chelly National Monument

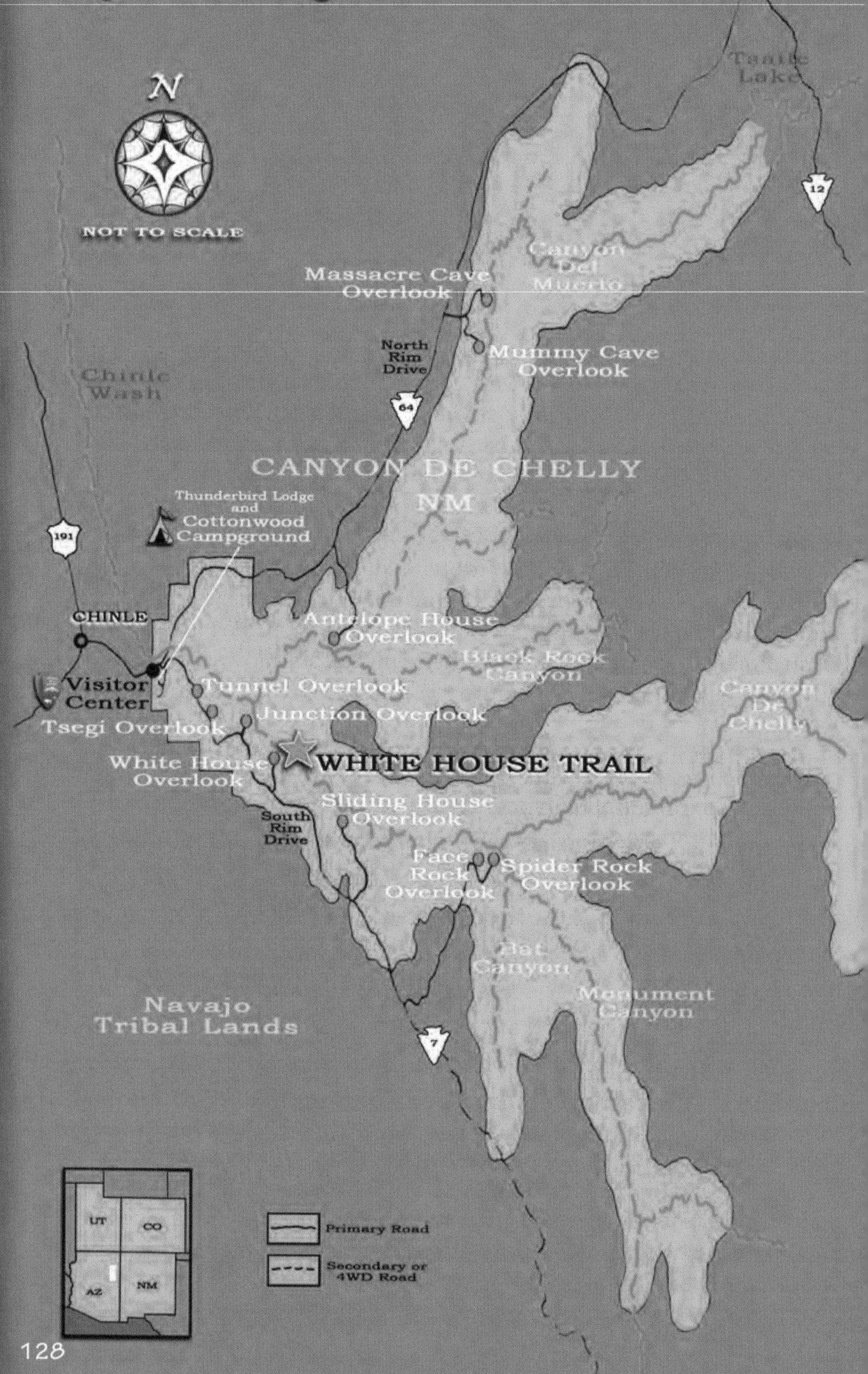

NOT TO SCALE

N

Taaie Lake

12

Chinle Wash

Massacre Cave Overlook

Canyon Del Muerto

Mummy Cave Overlook

North Rim Drive

64

CANYON DE CHELLY NM

Thunderbird Lodge and Cottonwood Campground

191

CHINLE

Antelope House Overlook

Black Rock Canyon

Canyon De Chelly

Tunnel Overlook

Visitor Center

Junction Overlook

Tsegi Overlook

★ **WHITE HOUSE TRAIL**

White House Overlook

Sliding House Overlook

South Rim Drive

Face Rock Overlook

Spider Rock Overlook

Navajo Tribal Lands

Bat Canyon

Monument Canyon

7

UT   CO

AZ   NM

————— Primary Road

- - - - - Secondary or 4WD Road

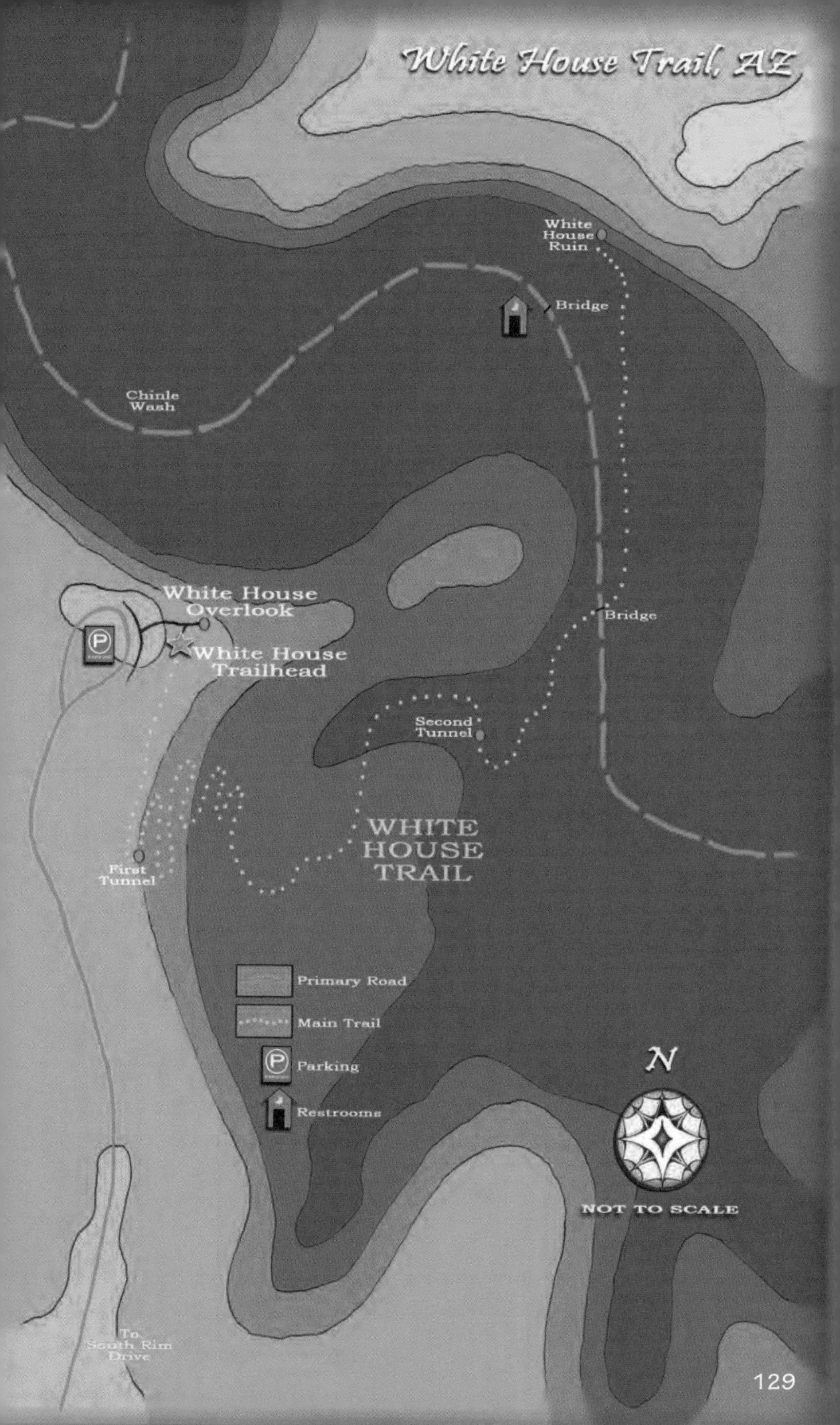

White House Trail, AZ

White House Ruin

Bridge

Chinle Wash

Bridge

White House Overlook

White House Trailhead

Second Tunnel

WHITE HOUSE TRAIL

First Tunnel

Primary Road

Main Trail

P Parking

Restrooms

N

NOT TO SCALE

To South Rim Drive

Chapter Three

Tips & Advice

I think back on the pleasures that I've had on the trail and the teachings that it has imparted to me, and how those pleasures and those teachings have given me happiness and a greater understanding of how to bring fullness and richness into my life.

Ann Sutton

An abstract of colored stone in Paria Canyon

The overall strategy when hiking the Colorado Plateau is always to plan ahead and know, literally, what you are getting into, and how to get back out. Make sure you carry enough food, protection from the elements, and especially water. It is also very important that everyone in your hiking group be physically and mentally prepared for the journey. Always be sure to check the local weather forecast, trail conditions, road closures, and water availability prior to heading into the backcountry. That said, what follows is my laundry list of other thoughts, ruminations, and recommendations for hikers and backpackers....

≈ General Hiking and Backpacking Tips:

✿ **Never go canyon exploring unprepared.** At the minimum, make sure you carry the ten essentials (see list on page 8). Ample water is a necessity. In summer months you have to employ a sound strategy for limiting exposure from the midday heat. Also, during the heat of summer, wear cotton clothing, since it stays wet longer and therefore keeps you cooler. For the cool season, wear fleece and synthetics that dry quickly. Always dress in layers.

✿ **Never hike alone.** As an experienced backpacker, I have hiked alone many a time in canyon country. That said, I strongly advise less seasoned hikers not to hike alone until gaining the proper experience. Statistics reveal that solo hikers make especially bad decisions when simple dehydration sets in. Also be sure to tell someone at home when to expect your return and what your itinerary is. Notify them when you get off trail to let them know you are safe and sound before they call out the cavalry.

✿ **Stay on the trails.** Never shortcut switchbacks. It causes erosion in a desert climate where plants have a difficult enough time getting established. Lack of vegetation, in turn, causes washouts on the trail during severe storms. Plus, such side trails may cause others to get lost. Also, keep your eyes on the trail. While you are hiking, your gaze should be glued to the trail just about three to six feet in front of you, with only quick glances further ahead to see what's coming up. You can take quick looks around, but try to keep your focus on the trail or you will inevitably trip.

✪ **Pack it in – pack it out.** Do not leave any trash in the backcountry. Repackaging your food can help to minimize waste. Before you leave your campsite, or when you take a break on the trail, check and make sure you haven't left any food, litter, or gear. Prior to heading out after a trail break make sure your pack is fully zipped and battened down. Once zippers start to open, they usually slide more, until they are wide open and you start dropping gear along the trail. In many popular and sensitive backcountry areas, you'll be required to pack out your poop too. Several commercial brands of human waste disposal systems are on the market nowadays and the agency requiring their use will usually provide them free of charge. Otherwise, I suggest you at least double or triple bag and seal it (no sense in risking having a popped poop parcel inside your pack).

✪ **Be extra cautious in summer heat.** When temperatures reach more than ninety degrees, make sure you are off the trail during the hottest time of day, usually between 10 a.m. and 4 p.m. Always drink plenty of fluids, and drink enough for the water to moisten the body's organs, not just little sips that wet your whistle. In summer heat you need to drink at least a quart of water and/or sport drink for every hour of hiking. Take breaks in shade every hour for about ten minutes; eat snacks (especially salty ones) and drink up. Try to take your time when you hike. Remember, the journey is your destination, so enjoy it.

✪ **Fed is dead.** Feeding human food to wildlife can alter their digestive systems and ultimately kill them. It is also illegal to approach or feed any of the wildlife within the National Park System, including deer or squirrels.

✪ **Think twice about having a backcountry fire.** In a few backcountry areas fires may be allowed, but try to refrain from using precious desert resources unless a campfire is necessary. If you need a fire, keep it small and use only wood gathered from the ground. Never rip limbs from live or standing trees, never burn your trash in the fire, and always check local fire restrictions, especially during times of high fire danger.

✪ **Pets are allowed in the developed areas** in most of the recreational parks mentioned in this book, but they must be on a leash at all times. As a general rule, pets are not allowed on hiking

Sliding House Overlook, Canyon de Chelly National Monument

trails, but check with each supervising authority before leaving your dog at home. There are exceptions, such as West Fork Trail and Buckskin Gulch, that do allow leashed pets on the trail, while at Bryce Canyon pets are not even allowed at viewpoints. So, you never know what the criteria may be. I love my pets dearly, but due to the hot and remote settings described in this book, I would suggest leaving them back home when possible.

✿ **Bicycles are generally allowed only on designated roads.** Bicycles should not be used to travel in washes, on hiking trails, or in the backcountry. They are not allowed in designated wilderness areas or on any of the trails listed in this book.

✿ **Graffiti is illegal.** Respect other hiker's rights to a natural experience. Don't carve your name on anything, draw or doodle on the rocks or restroom walls, or build structures of any kind. No one really wants to see someone's initials etched into the natural surroundings. You can be fined, and graffiti removal simply adds to the backlog of maintenance chores and expenses for each park or recreation area.

✿ **Respect artifacts and ruins.** Do not touch, remove, or disturb artifacts from historic mining or Native American ruins, including rock art sites. They are protected by state and federal laws and violators are prosecuted.

◎ *Side Step:*
Wilderness Ethics

Wilderness ethics are really simple common sense. We need to reduce our impact on these special places to ensure they will remain intact and available for the enjoyment of generations to come. So, whenever possible, stay on the trail, camp on durable surfaces, know local regulations, avoid having a backcountry fire, respect wildlife, do not build anything, and properly dispose of human waste. Whatever you pack in, pack out, including every little scrap of trash. Try to be relatively quiet and respect other visitors' rights to enjoy a quality natural experience. Leave wildflowers, rocks, and other natural objects alone. Or, as the Leave No Trace slogan says: "Remember to take only pictures and leave only footprints." Backcountry explorers for eons to come will be thankful.

✿ **No swimming in major rivers.** Many people have died trying to swim across the Colorado River since the current appears very passive. Unfortunately, once you have entered its cold, energy-sapping waters you can find yourself unable to escape its powerful flow as hypothermia quickly sets in, and you are ultimately swept downstream to your death. I know it sounds melodramatic, but it happens quite often. This warning also extends to many stretches of the San Juan, Green, and Little Colorado Rivers.

✿ **A bit of trail protocol:** The uphill hiker has right of way, but use common sense; many times the uphill hiker welcomes a quick rest stop. If horses or mule teams approach you from either direction, step off to the inside of the trail, stand quietly, and wait until the last animal is at least 50 feet past before reentering the trail. Do not get yourself into the position where you are teetering on the outside edge of the trail waiting for them to go by, and never reach out to "pet" a passing pack animal.

✿ **Respect other hikers trying to enjoy their natural environment.** Avoid yelling or making loud noises on the trail or at your campsite unless there is an emergency.

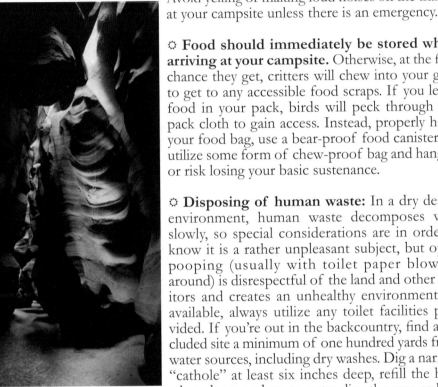

✿ **Food should immediately be stored when arriving at your campsite.** Otherwise, at the first chance they get, critters will chew into your gear to get to any accessible food scraps. If you leave food in your pack, birds will peck through the pack cloth to gain access. Instead, properly hang your food bag, use a bear-proof food canister, or utilize some form of chew-proof bag and hang it, or risk losing your basic sustenance.

✿ **Disposing of human waste:** In a dry desert environment, human waste decomposes very slowly, so special considerations are in order. I know it is a rather unpleasant subject, but open pooping (usually with toilet paper blowing around) is disrespectful of the land and other visitors and creates an unhealthy environment. If available, always utilize any toilet facilities provided. If you're out in the backcountry, find a secluded site a minimum of one hundred yards from water sources, including dry washes. Dig a narrow "cathole" at least six inches deep, refill the hole when done, and try to naturalize the area as best you can. Toilet paper should be carried out in a

Upper Antelope Canyon

double layer of zipper bags. Add a little baking soda in the bag to help control odors. Commercial "human waste disposal bags" (*a.k.a.* wag bags) are available for purchase at outdoor retailers and are required in many of the most-used wilderness areas.

Diarrhea is one of the most common ailments in the backcountry. Its root cause is almost always poor hygiene. Make sure you wash your hands after you go, use anti-bacterial hand sanitizers or hand wipes to keep contamination to a minimum, and try not to stick your dirty hands in your nose or mouth or eat food hand-to-mouth.

✪ **Locating desert water sources:** If you get into an emergency situation where you find yourself running out of water on a hike, you should first try to get out of the sun and limit your movement during the heat of the day. Cut down a bit on food intake too, as it diverts water for digestion that your body could use to help cool itself. Check your map to see if there is any identifiable water source close by. Look and listen for birds where you might locate their watering hole. Look for green vegetation or tall deciduous trees such as cottonwoods or other water-loving plants like willows, hackberry, salt cedar, and cattails, although you may have to dig around them a bit to find water. Water tends to pool in low-lying areas, rock depressions, and on the outer bend of dry river beds. If the soil feels damp just beneath the surface, dig a bit more and see if water seeps into it. Use a piece of fabric to soak up the moisture and wring it into your mouth: every little bit counts.

✪ **Using emergency communications:** Since the advent of cell phones, satellite phones, personal location beacons (PLBs), and satellite GPS messengers, various communication tools have been used extensively, and in most cases very successfully, in search-and-rescue situations. That said, emergency communication devices should never be relied upon in the backcountry. First of all, cell phones rarely work in the wilderness areas of the Colorado Plateau, and none of these units are intended to replace common sense, informed decision making, or training and trip planning.

Another wonderful view along Druid Arch Trail, Canyonlands National Park

Abuse in deploying these devices and initiating rescue missions has been growing, as emergency signals are being sent more often by novice backcountry visitors for non-life-threatening reasons. A reasonable person should know what they are getting into before entering the wilderness, and should be fully prepared physically and mentally for such a challenge. If a rescue is initiated, you may be charged the cost of the rescue, and in one instance I am aware of, a hiker was charged with "creating a hazardous condition" after calling for backcountry rescue three times in two days for various non-life-threatening situations.

✿ **Desert driving:** As a general rule, if you have a low-clearance vehicle you should probably remain on well-maintained roads. In wilderness areas, road maintenance occurs infrequently. When driving on unimproved surfaces, be particularly vigilant for potholes, deep ruts, sharp rocks, washouts, deep sand, and the like. One of the most common problems for drivers occurs after a rain when the roads become so "greasy" that you lose traction and fish-tail, or slide completely off the road. For this reason, many of the roads accessing trailheads referred to in this book are considered impassable when wet. You should always check with the agency managing the area concerning road conditions before entering wilderness areas.

 Side Step: Staying on the Desert Trail

Desert trails are notoriously difficult to follow. Hikers should be constantly observant and search ahead for common trail signs such as rock stacks, also known as cairns, which are most often used to direct hikers and help keep them safely on the trail. Another device used to keep folks on course is lining the trails' outer edges with stones or dead branches. Think twice before stepping over these impediments, even if you see foot-prints on the other side tempting you. You should also be careful to remain on the trail when crossing large expanses of open sandstone, or when following along dry streambeds, where trails can suddenly turn and climb out of the wash. On slickrock, look for cairns and a faintly lighter color worn into the rock surface from the thousands of others who have journeyed there before. As a general rule, unless mentioned specifically in your trail description, if you find yourself hand-over-hand climbing, then you are probably off the trail. Anytime you lose the trail, retrace your steps until locating the right path—99.99 percent of the time this will get you back on track. For the other 0.01 percent, it's time to break out the map and compass that I know you brought with you. Right?

Do not attempt to cross flooded washes. In Arizona they have a "stupid motorist law" where those who must be rescued after attempting to drive through flooded washes are required to pay for their rescue. Be careful parking your vehicle in streambeds or dry washes, especially during monsoon season, when a once-dry streambed can become a torrent that carries your vehicle away.

✿ **Physically preparing for your hike:** The most physically demanding hike in this book is the Hermit Trail in the Grand Canyon. The average hiking times from the South Rim to the Colorado River are about five to seven hours down and nearly double that coming out. This makes for a long day, and you must ensure that you are physically ready to endure this activity with proper preparatory exercise.

Begin your conditioning for any canyon excursion months in advance by doing step aerobics or hiking that involves enough elevation gain to steadily increase your heart rate, lung capacity, and muscle endurance. Start with short distances and increase the length of time for these aerobic activities. Simultaneously, start light and steadily increase the amount of weight you take on, working up to a minimum of half the weight you intend to carry. Of course, be sure to check with your doctor for advice before beginning a new exercise regimen.

Hurricane Wash in spring bloom

✿ **Shoes and foot protection:** Your shoes should be constructed of lightweight, flexible materials, and must be thoroughly broken-in before venturing into the canyon, or you risk getting blisters. For desert hiking, there is no need for heavy, full-leather, stiff-shank boots. I've read that every extra pound of weight on your feet equals almost five pounds on your back, so it pays to be weight conscious about what you wear on your feet.

One pair of mid- or heavy-weight socks should be worn. Some folks, like me, still use a lightweight inner sock for added cushioning. Socks should be made of wool or synthetic fabric since cotton keeps feet wet and encourages blistering. Trim your toenails a few days before your trip to prevent long nails from cutting into adjacent toes. This gives them time to heal in case you've trimmed them a little too close. I also wear short ankle gaiters to keep sand and rocks from getting into my shoes.

Indian Paintbrush and dead juniper

☼ **Water purification:** Many people see clear water in a wilderness area and, believing it is safe, freely drink from the creeks and rivers. What you can't see are things like giardia and cryptosporidium that can and will make you very sick. The most readily available method of purifying water for drinking and cooking is by boiling. This can be very time (and fuel) consuming, but heating water until it boils will kill anything harmful. Another choice is to use chemical treatments. These are small and easy-to-carry chemical tablets that, when mixed into the water and allowed their allotted time, kill most contaminates. I still use a water filter, sometimes combined with a UV treatment. Go for a lightweight system and ask your outdoor retailer for advice on which unit will work best for you. The newest forms of water treatment units are battery operated. Some use salt and electricity while others work by using an ultra-violet light system. Treatment systems should meet EPA guidelines.

☼ **Food basics:** I readily admit that I am no gourmet, but unless you really need to cook extravagant meals, stick to the basics. Dehydrated meals made especially for backpacking and good old ramen-type noodles should suffice for most meals. For breakfast, I take instant oatmeal or similar dehydrated mixes that require just a little hot water to prepare. If you back that up with your choice of energy and nutritional bars, trail mixes, crackers, cheese, peanut butter, dried fruit, or pretzels, then you should survive. Remember, the average hiker should consume about two pounds of food per day.

☼ **Choosing a backpack:** Internal frame packs are what most people use these days. They hug your back and have less side-to-side sway than external packs, giving you more stability. External frames keep the load off your back and provide some air flow between your back and the pack itself, making them a little cooler but slightly less stable from shifting loads. Externals allow you to walk more upright and are usually less expensive than internals but can be bulkier.

When backpacking, first of all, travel light. Food and water should be your two heaviest items, and you should carry only about one-third your total body weight when your backpack is fully loaded. When loading your backpack, make sure you pack most of the weight in the center of your back. This means that your heaviest item (usually the food bag) will be in the lower depths of your pack, so be sure to keep some nibble foods in a side pouch and handy for the trail.

138

The usual order I use in packing, from bottom to top: sleeping bag, tent, food, clothing, and miscellaneous gear. Water bottles should be readily accessible while hiking, and I always keep rain gear or extra clothing layers at the top of the pack for quick access. You can adjust your pack to your liking, but make sure it is balanced from side to side. Try not to have loose straps that can get snagged along the trail, and don't stack it too high or you could find yourself bouncing dangerously off of tree branches, rock overhangs, and the like.

With an internal frame pack, be very cautious not to put anything hard sticking into your back or stuff it to the point where it pushes the natural contoured shape of the pack out of kilter. The weight of your pack should ride on your hips. If the pack straps are cutting into your shoulders, tighten the hip belt around your waist or reach up to the straps near your ears and tighten the load lifters. Finally, avoid additional stress on the pack by only tightening the straps until they are taut. Excessive tightening will cause seams to rip and eventually pop open.

⚬ **Hiking sticks (trekking poles):** You'll hear some people call them ski poles and make disparaging comments, but they literally take tons of weight off your knees for each mile you hike. For the unparalleled stability they provide, most backpackers are much better off using them. Ask your outdoor retailer which style suits you best and get used to them while preparing for your hike. I like them for my back and knees, using them to lower myself slowly in lieu of taking the pounding during steep descents.

⚬ **Tents:** Purchase a good quality tent to ensure it actually keeps you dry when it rains, and remember to seal the seams if the manufacturer has not already done so. A good weight nowadays

---

◎ **Side Step:**
Elevation's Effect on Temperatures

Visitors to the American Southwest often believe temperatures along the plateau to be very fickle, as readings will quickly drop fifteen degrees or more, for example, when driving a mere 85 miles from Coyote Gulch Trailhead (at about 4,500 feet) to the Bryce Canyon Visitor Center (at 8,000 feet). Quite often, as in this example, the temperature fluctuation is simply due to the change in elevation. For every one thousand foot change in elevation, temperatures will change accordingly by about 3–5 degrees. In simple terms, this is due to the lower atmospheric pressure at higher elevations, causing the air molecules to move slower, cooling the ambient temperatures. Meteorologists use this fact to predict snow levels. If a winter storm is on the way, they will usually predict what elevation snow is to be expected. Paying close attention to the elevations where you'll be hiking can help you plan your clothing layers and camping gear.

The changeover to digital photography during the last decade has been phenomenal. Adaptive and versatile, these cameras have quickly replaced film cameras, and we no longer have to carry bags of film with us when we travel.

Most cameras work basically the same way. Turn it on, compose the scene, hold your breath and steady the camera. Most cameras utilize a shutter button with two stages. As you slowly press the shutter halfway down, the camera sets focus and exposure. Then you slowly press the shutter all the way down to take the picture.

When composing a shot, remember that photographic balance is very important. The arrangement of lines, colors, shapes, and areas of light and dark that complement one another make a photograph appear well-balanced. Generally we find asymmetrical balance more interesting to view than a stodgy and perfectly centered symmetrical balance. For improved composition, try the "rule of thirds" as a guide for placement of your subjects. Before you take a photo, imagine the picture area divided into thirds both horizontally and vertically. The intersections of these imaginary lines provide four options for the placement of the central interest of the photograph. The particular "third" you select depends upon the subject matter, but remember that in our culture we read photographs like we read text, from left to right, and something like a big rock placed in the left foreground can block visual entry into the photograph.

If possible, keep a filter, such as a UV filter or a polarizer, attached to your lens for protection.

The best times of day to photograph landscapes are around sunrise and sunset, during what is referred to as the "golden hour." Typically at this time, the light is softer (more diffuse) and warmer in hue, while shadows are lighter and longer. In the middle of the day, the bright overhead sun quite often turns landscapes flat with little shadow at all (referred to as "harsh-lighting"). Because the contrast is lower during the golden hour, shadows are less dark, and highlights are less likely to be overexposed. In landscape photography, the warm color of the low sun is often considered desirable to enhance the colors of the scene. Professional photographers plan for the golden hour by scouting possible locations for early morning and early evening shots.

A few other tips include using an interesting foreground, such as flowers, when employing a wide angle lens. (To keep the full scene in your photos sharp use a higher aperture setting of F16 or above.) If the scene is getting dark and you don't have a tripod, try adjusting your ISO settings to a higher number. The image can degrade a bit with high ISO settings, but this may be preferable to an otherwise blurry image. Remember, within any given scene there is always a potentially good photograph; you just have to find the right composition.

for a two-person tent is six pounds or less, and pieces can be divided up easily enough (one person takes the rain fly and poles, while the other carries the tent base). In the summer when no rain is expected, go without the rainfly to save weight. I use a one pound bivy bag for cool seasons, and a slightly lighter bug bivy in the warm season if no rain is expected. And of course, you can always go al fresco and lay out a tarp and sleep on top of it to have a clear view of the sky on starry nights.

✿ **Sleeping bags:** Down-filled bags are light and warm but can be expensive—and if they get wet, they lose their loft and are nearly useless. Synthetic bags will maintain some warmth when wet and are less expensive than down but will weigh a bit more. Remember to match the bag's warmth rating with the area's climate and current weather trends.

✿ **Know your local weather and what temperatures to expect.** Make sure you pack for the minimum and maximum temperatures you are likely to experience, and expect the worst case scenario. Temperatures get colder at higher elevations at a rate of about four degrees per 1,000 foot gain. For example, you can expect that inside the Grand Canyon along the Colorado River, at roughly 2,000 foot elevations, temperatures are about twenty degrees warmer than on the rim at an elevation of about 7,000 feet. In the dry western climate, temperature swings of fifty degrees between day and night are not uncommon. A comfortable seventy degrees when the sun is out at midday can dive down into the freezing range at night.

Annual precipitation along the Colorado Plateau averages about ten to twelve inches, with two distinct weather patterns. During the cool season (October 16 to April 15) frontal systems generated in the Pacific Ocean and Gulf of Alaska come in from California and Nevada, bringing cold winds and some precipitation. Save for the higher elevations, most snow storms deposit one to three inches of wet snow, which quickly melts away when the sun comes out.

The warm season (April 16 to October 15) brings a few Pacific storms until the heat builds and a strong high pressure system sets up over the Four Corners region. That triggers the monsoon season (June 15 to September 30), the wettest time of the year for most of canyon country, when nearly every afternoon, thunderstorms can occur, sometimes severe enough to generate flash floods.

Reflecting pools along West Fork Oak Creek in late fall

Average Monthly Temperatures

PARK:	Arches NP 5,000 feet	Grand Canyon NP Inner Canyon: 2,400 feet	Bryce Canyon NP 8,000 feet
Month	HI / LO	HI / LO	HI / LO
January	45 / 20	55 / 35	40 / 10
February	50 / 30	60 / 40	40 / 15
March	65 / 35	70 / 50	45 / 15
April	70 / 40	80 / 55	55 / 25
May	80 / 50	90 / 60	65 / 30
June	95 / 60	100 / 70	75 / 40
July	100 / 70	105 / 80	85 / 45
August	100 / 65	105 / 75	80 / 45
September	90 / 55	100 / 70	75 / 35
October	75 / 40	85 / 60	65 / 30
November	55 / 30	70 / 45	50 / 20
December	45 / 20	60 / 35	40 / 10

Average Monthly Precipitation

January	0.6"	0.7"	1.7"
February	0.65"	0.75"	1.4"
March	0.75"	0.8"	1.4"
April	0.8"	0.05"	1.2"
May	0.75"	0.35"	0.8"
June	0.45"	0.3"	0.6"
July	0.7"	0.85"	1.4"
August	0.8"	1.5"	2.2"
September	0.9"	1.0"	1.4"
October	1.15"	0.65"	1.4"
November	0.6"	0.45"	1.2"
December	0.45"	0.9"	1.6"

Sunrise Times　　Sunset Times

Arches	Date	Grand Canyon	Grand Canyon	Date	Arches
7:35 a.m.	January 1	7:35 a.m.	5:25 p.m.	January 1	5:05 p.m.
7:35 a.m.	January 15	7:30 a.m.	5:35 p.m.	January 15	5:20 p.m.
7:25 a.m.	February 1	7:25 a.m.	5:55 p.m.	February 1	5:40 p.m.
7:00 a.m.	February 15	7:10 a.m.	6:05 p.m.	February 15	5:55 p.m.
6:50 a.m.	*March 1	6:55 a.m.	6:20 p.m.	*March 1	6:10 p.m.
6:30 a.m.	*March 15	6:35 a.m.	6:30 p.m.	*March15	6:25 p.m.
6:00 a.m.	*April 1	6:10 a.m.	6:45 p.m.	*April 1	6:40 p.m.
5:40 a.m.	*April 15	5:55 a.m.	6:55 p.m.	*April 15	6:55 p.m.
5:20 a.m.	*May 1	5:35 a.m.	7:10 p.m.	*May 1	7:10 p.m.
5:05 a.m.	*May 15	5:20 a.m.	7:20 p.m.	*May 15	7:25 p.m.
4:55 a.m.	*June 1	5:10 a.m.	7:35 p.m.	*June 1	7:35 p.m.
4:50 a.m.	*June 15	5:20 a.m.	7:40 p.m.	*June 15	7:45 p.m.
5:00 a.m.	*July 1	5:15 a.m.	7:45 p.m.	*July 1	7:45 p.m.
5:05 a.m.	*July 15	5:20 a.m.	7:40 p.m.	*July 15	7:40 p.m.
5:20 a.m.	*August 1	5:35 a.m.	7:30 p.m.	*August 1	7:30 p.m.
5:30 a.m.	*August 15	5:45 a.m.	7:15 p.m.	*August 15	7:10 p.m.
5:50 a.m.	*September 1	5:55 a.m.	6:50 p.m.	*September 1	6:45 p.m.
6:00 a.m.	*September 15	6:05 a.m.	6:30 p.m.	*September 15	6:25 p.m.
6:15 a.m.	*October 1	6:20 a.m.	6:10 p.m.	*October 1	6:00 p.m.
6:30 a.m.	*October 15	6:30 a.m.	5:50 p.m.	*October 15	5:40 p.m.
6:45 a.m.	*November 1	6:45 a.m.	5:30 p.m.	*November 1	5:20 p.m.
7:00 a.m.	*November 15	7:00 a.m.	5:20 p.m.	*November 15	5:05 p.m.
7:15 a.m.	December 1	7:15 a.m.	5:15 p.m.	December 1	4:55 p.m.
7:30 a.m.	December 15	7:25 a.m.	5:20 p.m.	December 15	5:00 p.m.

All times are approximate and have been rounded off.
If you are planning to watch the sunrise or sunset be sure to arrive at your viewing point
at least fifteen minutes before these times.
*Times are Mountain Standard Time; add one hour for daylight time, when in use.

Chapter Four

Mishaps & Remedies

The canyon country does not always inspire love. To many it appears barren, hostile, repellent—a fearsome, mostly waterless land of rock and heat, sand dunes and quicksand, cactus, thornbush, scorpion, rattlesnake, and agoraphobic distances. To those who see our land in that manner, the best reply is yes, you are right, it is a dangerous and terrible place. Enter at your own risk. Carry water. Avoid the noonday sun. Try to ignore the vultures. Pray frequently.

Edward Abbey

At Grand Canyon National Park alone, about a dozen people perish and over two hundred fifty people are rescued from the Inner Canyon each year. The biggest dangers we face when exploring the backcountry, in ranked order, include drowning, unroped falls, heart attacks, lightning, hypothermia, mountain lions, bees, mosquitoes, overconfidence and lack of know-how, heat, snakes, avalanches, rock injuries, spiders, bears, and the assumption your technology will save you. Of course, most of these situations will probably never happen to you, and with proper preparation and a modicum of common sense you can lessen the chance of any of these problems occurring. However, little mishaps can and do happen, so it is best to plan ahead and be prepared for any eventuality.

Any good first-aid kit will include a first-aid booklet. You should take the time to read it thoroughly and practice before and even during your trip. In this chapter, I list the most common health and safety concerns that can occur while hiking and exploring these canyons and offer a modicum of advice to help you avoid getting into such troublesome situations or what to do in case those things do happen. This advice does not replace taking certified first-aid training. The National Outdoor Leadership School (NOLS) teaches wilderness first-aid courses throughout the country that provide excellent training. I've taken a few of their courses and recommend them highly.

In Any Situation…

Stay calm, take a deep breath, assess the situation, and take control. Do not rush in to help someone else before ensuring the scene is safe; adding another injured person will not help the situation. Do not move the victim unless their safety is in danger. Once everyone's safety is assured, then approach the victim and determine what has happened, or what is called the Mechanism of Injury (MOI). Talk to the victim; listen to get a general impression of the situation which could be anything from "I'll be all right," to "I think something's broken," to the victim being confused or unconscious. If you can, write down your assessment and keep a record of the victim's condition. Review your first-aid book for details on this initial assessment and always have at least one person remain with the victim if help is required.

Evacuation in most instances is only necessary for a broken leg, poisonous snakebite, or other severe life-threatening emergency, or if the hiker's condition will turn critical if required to hike out. A patient requiring rescue puts many other lives at risk, so this should only be considered as a last resort. You should also be reminded that the hiker requiring emergency evacuation may be charged the cost of their rescue.

Cactus flower in Havasu Canyon. Although the flowers are lovely, cactus spines can prove difficult to remove even with a good pair of tweezers.

Check the Patient's ABCs

(Use the first-aid book in your kit for complete details):

A. **Airway**—If the patient is conscious and choking, use the Heimlich maneuver to clear the obstruction. If unconscious and not breathing, check for obstructions in the mouth, and use the head-tilt, chin-lift method to open the airway (unless a spinal injury is suspected; then use the jaw-thrust method).

B. **Breathing**—Once you have opened the airway, put your ear over the patient's mouth. Looking at the chest and abdomen for movement, listen for sounds of breathing, and feel for air against your ear. If the patient is not breathing, you must initiate rescue breathing.

C. **Circulation and bleeding**—Listen for a heartbeat and check for a pulse. If none, initiate CPR. Next, while wearing protective gloves, check for bleeding. Visually inspect the patient and run your hand under bulky clothing, checking your hand for any sign of blood. To control bleeding, apply direct pressure with the palm of your hand and elevate the wound if possible.

D. **Disability**—If you suspect a lower limb fracture, a spinal injury (most noticeably marked by immobility or tingling in hands or feet, for which you would stabilize the patient's head and keep their neck from moving), or any other life threatening emergency, send someone for help as soon as possible while you stay with the victim. Make sure the messenger knows the exact location and the complete nature of the injury or situation.

E. **Exposure**—Keep the patient comfortable, sheltered from rain and cold, and treat for shock.

Navajo Trail in Bryce Canyon. Due to the number of falls when tourists have attempted to ascend this crumbly rock, no climbing is allowed in this park.

≋ Specific Issues

✪ Blisters

Problem: Blisters are really burns caused by friction. Although they can be extremely painful, the main medical concern is infection. You can expect to get blisters unless special precautions are taken to avoid them.

Avoidance: Wear shoes that are well broken in, use blister-blocking adhesives, treat hot-spots immediately, and change into a pair of dry socks during the hike to help you avoid blisters.

Treatment: Using a sterile pin or knife, open a small hole in the blister and massage the fluid out. *Spenco 2nd Skin* works best for covering blisters; otherwise, cut a "donut" hole into a moleskin and apply it so the blister is exposed through the hole. Put a small amount of antibiotic ointment in the hole and cover it with another bandage.

✪ Cardiac Arrest

Problem: The symptoms usually include chest pain, shortness of breath, nausea and vomiting, and pale sweaty skin, among others.

Avoidance: Most hikers who have heart attacks on the trail have a previous condition that can be exacerbated by the strenuous activity. If you have a prior heart condition, make sure you have trained adequately for this arduous hike and get clearance from your doctor.

Treatment: General treatment includes keeping the airway open; keeping the patient still, calm, and comfortable; initiating CPR as needed; and arranging rapid evacuation.

✪ Dehydration/Heat Stroke

Problem: After blisters, this is the most common malady for canyon hikers during the summer months, bar none. The symptoms usually progress as water loss increases. Remember that the human body is 60 percent water and a hiker during summer heat can lose 20 percent (or about 12–18 pounds) of that water in one day of hiking. The chronological order of heat-related injury for the average person goes like this; after sweating about 2 precent of your body weight your thirst mechanism is triggered, at 3 percent your performance is reduced by about 10 percent, around 3–4 percent and heat exhaustion sets in. Then, at about 5 percent, your body begins losing a severe amount of muscle strength and endurance, and you begin to make really bad decisions. By the time your body has lost 6–9 percent of its water weight, incapacitation sets in and you are unable to stand. Next comes the onset of total delirium and coma—when you reach 20 percent you are gone. Initial symptoms include headache, pale and sweaty skin, cramps, nausea and vomiting, and fatigue. If you are not treated, your skin will turn red and hot and you will soon become disoriented, irritable, combative, and ultimately unconscious.

Avoidance: Start drinking extra water a few days before your trip and drink sport drinks with electrolytes a couple of hours before you begin your hike and while on the trail. Sport drinks containing electrolytes help keep your body chemistry balanced when sweating a lot. Especially in the summer season, you will need to drink a minimum of a quart of water and/or sport drink for every hour of hiking, and a total of more than two gallons per day. Drink enough fluids so that your urine runs clear. You can test if you are getting dehydrated by pinching the skin on your forearm. If you are properly hydrated, it should spring right back. Rest often while hiking and when it's hot, and take a break during the heat of midday (10 a.m.–4 p.m.). Wear light-colored, lightweight, well-ventilated clothing, and wear a hat for shade and heat protection. Avoid alcohol and caffeine, and consult your physician if you're taking antihistamines or antidepressants.

Treatment: Rest in a cool, shady spot. Slowly drink copious amounts of water and/or sport drinks. If possible, use some water to cool your head, hands, and feet. If symptoms progress, aggressive cooling is required; spray the victim with cool water and fan him or her while massaging muscle cramps, if needed. Evacuate if the victim is incapacitated.

✿ Drowning

Problem: The Colorado River appears to slowly meander through the Southwest, and many people don't realize what a huge amount of water flows within its narrow constraints. Especially during the hotter seasons, some people think they'll just jump in and cool off for a minute—and then are swept to their death downstream. If they survive long enough to climb out of the river, they are faced with the deadly chore of trying to find a way out of these canyon lands with no supplies, when trails are few and very far between.

Avoidance: NEVER attempt to swim the Colorado River (or its other major tributaries), nor go into the water much more than ankle deep. Along most other smaller creeks and rivers, exercise extreme caution if you decide to enter the water.

Treatment: If the victim is unconscious, check breathing and initiate rescue breathing if necessary. Check for a pulse and initiate CPR if necessary. The victim should be evacuated as soon as possible.

✿ Falls and Sprains

Problem: It will do you well to remember that in any direct fall of over twenty feet you will break something, or sustain a spinal or head injury. It is impossible to review fully, in this little guide, the myriad of traumatic injuries that can occur from a fall.

Avoidance: Do not climb canyon walls unless you are highly trained. Even then, while in a remote wilderness setting, I would not

◎ *Side Step*: Cairns (KAY-urns)

Cairns are man-made stacks of rocks constructed as a landmark. Cairns are found the world over and have been used since prehistoric times as markers and tombstones. The word originates from the British Isles, where cairns were often used in burial rituals, prompting numerous storied legends and folklore. For our purposes, cairns are the most widely used trail marker you are likely to encounter on any given trail. They can range from a couple of stacked rocks to three-foot-tall, heavy-gauge wire baskets filled with rocks. Placed at regular intervals, they indicate the trail's direction or can signal trail junctions. In North America, trail cairns can also be called "ducks" when they include a rock "bill" pointing in the trail's direction.

Trail cairn, Bear Mountain, Sedona

put myself in a situation where these types of injuries could occur. When hiking, keep your eyes and concentration on the trail or you could easily trip and go tumbling butt over teakettle, injuring yourself and possibly others.

Treatment: For simple sprains, RICE it. The acronym stands for Rest, Ice, Compression, and Elevation. So rest the injury, apply ice or cold on the swelling, wrap it, and elevate the sprain. Ice should remain on the site of the injury for no more than twenty minutes. As already stated, the list of possible sprains, fractures, and other blunt-force trauma that can happen from a fall are too numerous to be covered here. Please refer to your first-aid book for specific treatment; initiate the patient ABCs and evacuate as needed.

✪ Flash Flood

Problem: Flash floods kill more people each year in the United States than any other natural disaster. Recently a fellow photographer and experienced canyon backpacker died in a flash flood along with his hiking companion. In canyon country's steep, hard rock terrain, any rainstorm is capable of producing flash floods at any time of year, but during the summer monsoon season from late June to mid-September,

Slickrock areas of sandstone are not usually slick at all, unless there is a thin coating of sand on its surface, or when it rains (or snows).

be especially aware that afternoon thunderstorms are common, and the heavy downpours related to these storms are those most likely to produce flash floods.

Avoidance: Be cautious and stay away from creekbeds, dry washes, and narrow canyons, especially in afternoons during monsoon season and during any rainstorm. If you hear or see a flood coming, immediately climb to higher ground. Never try to outrun it!

Treatment: Drowning and general trauma are the usual injuries resulting from a flash flood; treat the victim accordingly, initiate the Patient ABCs, and evacuate as needed.

✪ Getting Lost

Problem: Most of the hikes listed in this book are pretty straightforward, as long as you pay proper attention and focus on the trail while using your map, compass, and trail description to keep you on track. All the same, I have seen people purposely leave the trail and attempt climbing up a wash, causing them to miss the trail completely. I have also seen people so engrossed in their conversation that they started descending a loose rock wash instead of the trail. These situations can cause an injurious fall or set a serious rockslide in motion that careens down to injure other hikers.

Avoidance: As a general rule, if you are hiking downcanyon, and you have a choice in direction where there is a fork in the trail, the main trail will nearly always descend, and vice-versa if traveling upcanyon. Always stay on the trail and never shortcut switchbacks. If the trail peters out, stop immediately, turn around, and retrace your steps back to the main trail. If you see a spur trail where you must step over branches or rocks to gain access, more than likely you've just stepped off the main trail. When the trail is faint, look for cairns (rock stacks) to guide you. On slickrock you can usually see a worn path of a slightly lighter color than its surroundings. Otherwise, follow whatever tracking information is present, including dirt trails, footprints, tree blazes (marks cut into a tree's bark), and any available signage.

Treatment: Prepare by studying maps and trail descriptions before and during your hike. Learn basic compass and navigational skills prior to the trip. If you are totally and hopelessly lost, stay calm and stay put, using your whistle or signal device to let rescuers and others know where you are. Please note: I purposely did not include GPS (Global Positioning System) coordinates in this book since most trails described here are well signed and can easily be done without a GPS. Furthermore, in slot canyons, satellite reception can be spotty at best.

✿ Hypothermia

Problem: It's been reported that hypothermia could be related to more backcountry injuries and deaths than any other cause. Basically, if your body loses heat faster than it can be produced, your core temperature will begin to plummet, and you'll begin to completely lose your head. Symptoms usually start with a loss of fine motor skills, and total lack of judgment, followed by uncontrolled shivering, and cold, pale skin. As this condition progresses, the victim stops shivering and ultimately loses consciousness.

Avoidance: Wear clothing layers that retain heat when wet. Be aware that cotton holds no heat when wet and stays wet for a long time, thus the cliché, "cotton kills." Use rain gear during inclement weather and change into warm, dry clothes before getting chilled. Drink lots of water, eat plenty of carbs, and rest often.

Treatment: Get the patient warm, dry, and sheltered from wind and rain. Make sure the head and neck are covered to prevent heat loss and have him or her drink a warm (not hot) beverage. The old remedy is to use direct body contact to warm the victim, but this has recently been dismissed in lab tests. Instead, use heat packs or hot water bottles applied to the palms and soles, (but not directly on the skin), and get the patient wrapped into a sleeping bag, insulated from the ground, with added layers for extra warmth. Evacuate if necessary.

✿ Illness

Problem: In this broad category, I'll quickly cover common illnesses such as headache, diarrhea, muscle ache, and sunburn. These are some of the usual maladies that can happen while hiking, and I have experienced many myself, including, a twenty-four hour stomach virus the night before hiking out of the backcountry.

Avoidance: Many illnesses can be difficult to avoid, but contributing factors like overexertion, a pack that's too heavy, and over exposure to the sun are avoidable. Make sure you cover any exposed skin with either clothing or sunscreen and wear a wide-brimmed hat when out in the sun. (Anytime I hike the Grand Canyon I wear a "foreign legion" style hat with a large bill and a cape to cover my neck.)

Bouts of stomach illness are most often caused by poor hygiene. Make sure you wash your hands thoroughly after using the toilet, and use anti-bacterial wipes or gel sanitizers to help minimize exposure. Avoid putting your dirty hands in your nose or mouth, or eating food hand-to-mouth, and when you sneeze, direct your sneeze into your elbow, not onto your germ-spreading hands. To limit your risk, you should also refrain from sharing things like trail mix, lip balm, or eating utensils, and don't let the sick person in your group do the cooking for the rest of the party.

Treatment: For headache and muscle aches, rest, drink water or sports beverages, massage the muscles, and take a nonsteroidal anti-inflammatory (NSAID) such as ibuprofen. When sunburned, limit any added exposure, cool the skin, apply aloe or a skin moisturizer, and take ibuprofen. If you experience a bout of diarrhea, it is especially important to stay hydrated, so drink water and electrolyte-type sport drinks, and take an over-the-counter medication if necessary. Oral rehydration salt solutions can be found in packet form at most outdoor retailers. These are best used for fighting the worst cases of diarrhea, and although their taste is not very appealing, be sure to include them in your first-aid kit.

As to my case of stomach virus, I had diarrhea, vomiting, and a mild fever all night. I kept myself hydrated using water with a little oral rehydration salts mixed in and, after most of the diarrhea had run its course, I took Imodium (as I prefer to get the virus out of my system prior to taking something to stop the diarrhea). Since I hadn't slept, I crashed out in camp during the day, ate some oatmeal, drank until I could drink no more, took some aspirin, and headed up the trail late that afternoon. It wasn't the most fun I've had, but you do what needs to be done.

○ Lightning

Problem: Second only to flash floods, lightning kills more people each year in the Unites States than any other weather-related incident. A single bolt can carry as much as 200 million volts and can strike a person up to ten miles away from the storm front.

Avoidance: Make yourself familiar with local weather patterns such as the Southwestern summer monsoon season that ushers in afternoon thunderstorms. Avoid hiking in exposed locations like cliff edges or being near isolated tall objects like trees and metal poles during these and other stormy times. In order to monitor a storm front, remember that sound carries at one mile per five seconds, so if you count the number of seconds after you see a flash of lightning and divide it by five, you'll know about how far away the storm is. If you get caught in a lightning storm, move to a low area that does not collect water, take off your pack, and squat low on your sleeping pad if possible (for insulation). In your tent, stay on your sleeping pad and do not touch the tent walls. If at any time you feel the hair rise on the back of your neck, get down quickly!

Treatment: A lightning strike can accost you in many ways—a direct strike, ground current, and the blast effect, to name a few. Because of the myriad ways you can be injured (cardiac arrest, burns, respiratory arrest, neurological injury, and other trauma), you should initiate the Patient ABCs as soon as the scene is secure and evacuate as necessary.

✧ Mountain Lions

Problem: Mountain lions, or cougars, are extremely elusive and you should count yourself lucky if you ever spot one of these splendid animals in the wild. The only time I have ever seen cougar footprints was in mud along Water Holes Canyon outside Page, Arizona, some years ago. Since the 1970s an average of about three people have been killed every decade from cougar attacks, half of them children. However rare an attack is, cougar assaults can prove fatal unless precautions are taken.

Avoidance: Hike with a companion or a group, and be alert for signs of cougar activity such as tracks or the scent of an animal carcass. If you face a cougar, stay calm. Do not approach the animal, and make sure you provide an avenue for the cougar to escape. Try to make yourself appear larger and talk in a soothing and confident voice. Do not run, make sudden movements, or turn your back on the animal. Pick up and protect any small children. If the cougar appears aggressive, throw rocks (if you can pick one up

Drowning is always a concern, even in the gorgeous blue-green waters of Havasu Creek, seen here reflecting the canyon walls at sunset.

without crouching down and making yourself appear smaller), bang pans, and use a stick or hiking staff to defend yourself if need be. If attacked, fight back aggressively and use anything at your disposal to defend yourself and others.

Treatment: Cougar attacks can produce lacerations and puncture wounds (bites). Stop any bleeding, rinse the injury with clean water, and bandage wounds with a sterile dressing. Unless the wounds are deemed superficial scratches, evacuate the patient immediately, regardless of the severity of those injuries.

✿ Rock Slides

Problem: Rock slides occur quite often in the canyons of the Colorado Plateau and have the potential to be deadly. Due to the amount of loose rock along cliffs and in drainages, these canyons are ripe for this type of occurrence.

Avoidance: Do not stand or rest in obvious slide areas. Stay on the trail and do not shortcut switchbacks, as you can loosen debris and cause rock slides to rain down on those below you. Listen for rock slides, particularly after severe storms. I've seen one rock slide along Hermit Trail—it sounded like a far off jet plane at first, and then turned into the classic rock-tumbling noise I remembered from movies.

Treatment: Injuries will vary, so treat the victim accordingly. Initiate the Patient ABCs and evacuate as needed.

The western diamondback is one of many rattlesnake species that makes its home in the desert Southwest. (NPS Photo)

☼ Snake and Insect Bites

Problem: The Colorado Plateau does harbor a few poisonous critters. The ones you should be most wary of are black widow and brown recluse spiders, scorpions, and rattlesnakes. While these are some of the most venomous creatures in the country, you'll find that if you ever encounter any of them while in the canyon, they usually scurry away. It's only by being careless that you risk injury.

Avoidance: Don't handle any of these critters. I've read that in Tucson, Arizona, at least one person each year is rushed to the hospital when he is struck by a rattlesnake as he tries to kiss it. Not smart. Don't stick your hands or feet into or under anything where you can't see— bushes, brush, dark corners, etc. Leave your tent zipped up tightly, and check your boots and any clothing left outside your tent before putting them on. At night (critters' preferred time for moving about), wear shoes and use a flashlight while you are up and about.

For identification purposes, a black widow is jet black with a red hourglass on her abdomen. A brown recluse is usually reddish to light brown, with inch-long thin legs, and the shape of a violin is on the top of its body, with the head of the "fiddle" pointing towards the tail (although they are rarely found in canyon country). A scorpion is colored between light brown and yellow straw, about an inch to three inches long, pincers in front and a long tail, curled at the end, holding its stinger. A rattlesnake is a snake with rattles—stay away from it. I've rarely seen a rattlesnake while hiking in canyon country, but extra care must always be taken to avoid a strike. In most cases, you will hear the rattle long before you can see the snake. If you hear the buzz of a rattler, freeze immediately and without moving your head (if possible) locate the snake with your eyes. Once the snake relaxes from a striking position, slowly move away. If you are within about three feet of the snake, you are in striking distance. Slowly and carefully double that distance and you should be well out of its striking range.

Treatment: Most spider bites are initially painless, with intense pain setting in within ten to twenty minutes. Although patients may think they are dying, only a few people in the United States die from spider bites each year, while thousands are bitten. Common symptoms are

 Side Step : Slickrock

Slickrock is a term loosely used for large tracts of wind-polished sandstone presenting a fairly level surface to walk on. The name is usually a misnomer since the surface of most sandstone is not slick at all, but gritty like sandpaper, which provides excellent traction. That is, until it rains. When it gets wet, that same abrasive sandstone can become very slick as loose silty granules morph into something akin to slippery clay.

cramping, fever, chills, and nausea. General treatment is to wash the site and apply an antiseptic, apply a cold compress, administer pain killers, and evacuate.

On the other hand, a scorpion's sting hurts right away and can feel like a bad bee sting or worse. Death usually only occurs from severe allergic reaction, so if you are allergic to bee stings and are stung by a scorpion use the epinephrine (EpiPen) you should be carrying to prevent anaphylaxis. I've been stung many times by scorpions, and it's never been a big deal. Cooling the sting site is the best treatment, but if the victim has difficulty swallowing, heavy sweating, blurred vision, or other such troublesome signs, evacuate them immediately.

If you or a hiking companion is bitten by a rattlesnake, quickly move away from the snake and stay calm. The area of the bite may swell dramatically, so remove any tight clothing or jewelry. Nearly a third of rattlesnake bites are nonvenomous, "dry" bites, but you'll need to assume the worst, so clean the wound, and evacuate the patient as soon as possible. Do not use a Sawyer Extractor or other snakebite kit, as it has been shown that they do little good and can cause more damage to the tissue around the area of the bite. Do not apply cold, do not administer pain killers, do not give alcohol to the victim, and don't apply a tourniquet. Immobilize and splint the wound, then evacuate.

✧ Water Intoxication (Hyponatremia)

Problem: This heat-related illness can happen when you drink a lot of water without eating anything. Doing so may cause an imbalance of electrolytes so severe that you could end up suffering a seizure, a coma, or even death. Although this condition is really the opposite of dehydration, the symptoms are nearly identical—disorientation, nausea, vomiting, and fatigue.

Avoidance: Don't drink just water alone. Mix in some electrolyte-containing sports drinks. To help in avoiding hyponatremia, you'll also need to eat more than your normal intake of food, especially high-sodium foods, while hiking the canyon lands during seasonal heat.

Treatment: Rest and eat salty foods. If symptoms progress, monitor the victim's breathing and protect him or her during possible seizures. Even if you recognize the symptoms and treat this condition right away, the victim may need to be evacuated.

✧ Quicksand

Problem: First of all, there are very few places along these hikes where one might come upon an area of quicksand, although one of them is Buckskin Gulch. Second of all, don't panic; quicksand is very difficult to get out of, but it will not suck you under like in the movies since the density of quicksand will not allow you to sink—humans are simply too buoyant. Death in quicksand might come about if an unlucky solo hiker were to get inexorably stuck in the mire and succumb to dehydration or starvation.

Avoidance: Since quicksand is a combination of clay, sand, and water, it is virtually imperceptible, and therefore difficult to avoid. Hiking sticks can help test the firmness of the trail in front of you, and hiking in a group of two or more is always recommended as others can assist if you become ensnared in the muck and mire.

Treatment: Quickly remove your pack and lie on your back. Arch your back and spread your arms and legs, increasing your surface area and buoyancy. Begin wiggling your legs to loosen the suction, and then slowly and gradually swim-crawl your way out toward solid ground. The only real medical problem related to getting stuck in quicksand is muscle strains from struggling against the suction. If subjected to a pulled muscle, you should massage the affected area and RICE it (rest, ice, compression, elevation) as necessary.

Unroped falls account for a large number of hiking fatalities. Angels Landing in Zion Canyon has been the site of many such mishaps. (View from the top of the landing looking north toward the Narrows.)

Chapter Five

Fauna & Flora

The earth's vegetation is part of the web of life in which there are intimate and essential relations between plants and earth, between plants and other plants, between plants and animals. Sometimes we have no choice but to disturb these relationships, but we should do so thoughtfully, with full awareness that what we may do may have consequences remote in time and place.

Rachel Carson

With ubiquitous photographs of Southwestern rock formations indelibly etched into their minds, people understandably believe that this hard, harsh, hot place would be very sparse of life. Yet nothing could be further from the truth. This magical plateau contains about eighteen distinct ecosystems, everything from urban and agricultural zones, to alpine areas, to varied grasslands, to rare and exquisite wetland environs. Because of its geographical location, its varied topography and elevations, and its relatively roadless expanses, the Colorado Plateau is a land of extraordinary plant and animal diversity.

The Colorado Plateau is commonly referred to as a cold desert due to its average elevation of over 5,000 feet above sea level. Summer heat can be deadly, with high temperatures frequently exceeding 100 degrees in the shade, and winter often sees snow flying, although accumulation is usually minimal. The Great Basin, with its intermittent dry mountains and valleys, sits to the west of the plateau, while to the east, the Rocky Mountains provide a lush environment of high peaks and abundant forests. Thus, the regional biota includes a mixture of those communities, as well as a large number of native species that have evolved in isolated eco-islands. The plateau supports an extensive number of plants found nowhere else on the planet—over three hundred endemic species. And no other area of the country holds more diversity of mammals, with well over one hundred different species residing along its vast expanse.

≈ Ecosystems

An ecosystem consists of a complex web of interactions and relationships among interrelated living organisms. Organisms living in an ecosystem are dependent on the other species and organic structures residing within the ecological community. Any component exponentially growing or shrinking will have an impact on the whole environment. What follows is a closer look at a few of the more significant habitats of the plateau's eighteen ecosystems.

One of the most widespread is the **saltbush-grass** ecosystem comprising over 20 percent of the plateau's land area. It is dominated by several varieties of saltbush, the most common being the four-wing saltbush, an important food source for many animals. Broom snakeweed and

A large area of sagebrush in Red Canyon, UT

Indian ricegrass also make up a large part of this ecosystem. (It must be noted that grasslands are present in all representative ecosystems with dominant varieties varying according to the environmental conditions and elevations.)

Pinyon-Juniper Woodlands make up another 20 percent of the landscape along the plateau. Plant communities within these woodlands have developed a tolerance for both cold and drought conditions. Three varieties of juniper grow in the lower elevations of this ecosystem, usually in open areas with no significant understory shrubs. Juniper's scaly foliage helps it conserve water more efficiently than pinyons. Pinyon pines dominate the higher elevations, at times forming tight canopies that are often mixed with small oak, mountain mahogany, and sparse grasses.

The next largest ecosystem is dominated by **blackbrush**, a two- to three-foot bush growing in shallow soils. Blackbrush occurs more on the eastern side of the plateau, growing along drainages and valleys at elevations around 3,500–6,000 feet. Its name is due to the color its stems turn after rainstorms. Few animals will eat the plant, but it is the winter mainstay for bighorn sheep. Blackbrush often grows in monocultures with a scattering of Mormon tea and other grasses, primarily galleta and Indian ricegrass.

Sagebrush-grass ecosystems are diverse habitats that can dominate an area or, conversely, be intermingled within other ecosystems.

A pinyon-juniper habitat can be seen here in the foreground. Riparian-loving cottonwood trees are in the center with Cathedral Rock, Sedona, in the background.

Forbs (green, broad-leafed plants) and other trees and shrubs are also representative of this zone. This particular ecosystem covers over 43 million acres across the Western United States and Canada, making it one of the largest in North America.

Those rare areas along the plateau that remain moist perennially, or that flood seasonally, or that maintain a water supply beyond what is supplied by rainfall (usually during the growing season) are defined as **wetlands**. Wetlands include lakes, streams, creeks, springs, marshes, and riparian areas adjacent to wetlands. For obvious reasons, an enormous number of plants and animals in the desert are dependent on wetlands for their survival. To highlight the importance of wetlands, they represent less than one percent of total acreage of western public lands but support 70 to 90 percent of the total bird and animal life.

Making up another small but significant portion of the landscapes along the plateau, mountain-related ecosystems include about five separate ecosystems. These include high alpine, aspen, ponderosa, spruce-fir, and mountain brush ecosystems. **High alpine** zones are the harsh peaks at only the highest elevations of the plateau. Due to strong winds most plants tend to stay low and hug the ground. These isolated areas epitomize the concept of eco-islands as being unique environments.

Other mountain ecosystems are named for their dominant plant cover. Gray-white barked **aspens** can form luxuriant groves that glow a bright yellow-orange in autumn. Found between 7,500 and 10,500 feet, this ecosystem is important to many wildlife species. Tall **ponderosa** pines grow at elevations from 6,000–8,000 feet and are especially dominant in areas of Northern Arizona. Their distinctive bark is a colorful mix of red, orange, and light brown with mostly vertical "veins" of dark brown. **Spruce-fir** communities occur from 8,000–10,000 feet and require rich, moist soil. Mixed **mountain brush** ecosystems range from 5,000–8,000 feet and can include small oaks, maples, and mountain mahogany. These regions also contain grasslands and meadows, so important to a diverse collection of birds and animals.

All of the ecosystems along the Colorado Plateau are under stress, threatened from a wide variety of causes: the invasion of exotic vegetation, intensive livestock grazing, road use and development, natural resource extraction, altered fire patterns, human encroachment, and climate change. Reports suggest that nearly 20 percent of the plants and animals associated with sagebrush lands alone may be at risk of annihilation, truly a sad commentary on our responsibility as stewards of this majestic land.

The streaks you see flowing down and staining numerous canyon walls are referred to as desert varnish. Desert varnish occurs mainly where occasional water runoff cements dust particles (predominantly clay) to the wall, as microorganisms remove manganese from the rock face, oxidizes it, and adheres back onto the rock surface. The colors of the

varnish can include beautiful shades of white, yellow, red, black, and blue-gray, depending on the amount and proportion of the manganese and iron contained in the varnish. Smooth rock surfaces and the arid Southwest climate allow a particular varnish bacterium to thrive, although it can still take up to 10,000 years for full-fledged coatings to form.

Common Plants and Animals of the Colorado Plateau

∼ Mammals (over 100 species)

Since the pioneers began settling the plateau during the late 1840s the number of mammal species inhabiting the region has remained relatively stable. Species that have been abolished from the area include the grizzly bear, gray wolf, black-footed ferrets, lynx, wolverines, river otters, and wild bison. A few of the more common or interesting mammals you might see, if you are lucky enough, while traveling around the plateau are:

✿**Deer Mouse**: These small (3–4 inch long) mice are the most widespread in the country. This little guy prefers the lower elevation tree, shrub, and grasslands over riparian communities. Deer mice are sharply bicolored with brown on top and a white underbelly, and have black eyes and large ears. During a wet springtime, their populations can explode, triggering an outbreak of Hantavirus, a respiratory disease that can kill humans. The disease is usually spread by inhaling dust containing the mouse's dried urine or excrement. (Something you should be aware of if camping where mouse droppings are present.)

Ringtail: These nocturnal climbers can be found throughout the Southwest, as far north as Oregon and east to Kansas. Dark brown or gray-buff colored with large ears, white around their large eyes, and cat-like facial features, they can grow over two feet in length (including their namesake black-and-white striped tails, which are nearly as long as their bodies). Ringtails are excellent at climbing almost everything, including vertical rock walls. They live in rocky cliffs and caves, usually within a half-mile of a water source. True omnivores, they will eat almost anything including bugs, snakes, fruit, mice, and birds. Often referred to as ringtail cats, they are actually members of the raccoon family.

Desert Cottontail and Black-Tailed Jackrabbit: Both the desert cottontail and the black-tailed jackrabbit reside along the plateau and are most active at dawn and dusk. With similar diets of grass, leaves, twigs, and cactus, both species range in similar areas of woodlands, grasslands, and deserts. The smaller of the two is the cottontail, at about 15 inches, while jackrabbits can be closer to 22 inches long, with backsides that appear "jacked up." These rabbits are brownish-gray, though the cottontail has a whiter belly and the jackrabbit has its signature black tail and black-tipped ears. The jackrabbit, more adapted to extreme desert heat, uses its huge ears to regulate its body temperature more effectively than cottontails. Plus, the jack's longer legs mean it can run in bursts up to about 35 miles per hour, 20 miles an hour faster than the cottontail. Both are an important food source for local predators.

Mountain Lion: Speaking of predators, the mountain lion is the largest wildcat in North America (well over 100 pounds) and has the largest range of any mammal in the Western Hemisphere, from Canada to Argentina. Like other large predators, they were hunted nearly to extinction but survived by their elusive nature, plus the fact they do not eat carrion, and therefore did not eat poisoned meat meant for them. Mountain lions, also called cougars or pumas, are solitary carnivores, and individuals can have large ranges, from 10 to 350 square miles.

Mountain Lion (NPS Photo)

These lions may follow hikers but more out of curiosity, since attacks on humans are still extremely rare. Read more about mountain lions and how to protect yourself if you should encounter this splendid animal in the wild on page 154.

✿**Bobcat**: These medium-sized predators are usually twice the size of a domestic cat but can take down prey up to eight times their weight. Although these highly adaptable animals reside throughout the plateau, they are such stealthy creatures that they are rarely seen. It helps that they are primarily nocturnal. Bobcats are solitary and territorial, using stalk-and-ambush methods to hunt prey. Their diet consists mostly of rodents and birds, and occasionally, deer. Although they were hunted in the past for their fur, they were resilient enough to survive and have rebounded in large numbers throughout the United States.

✿**Mule Deer**: Since most of its predators have been eliminated, mule deer populations have soared. They now reside throughout the plateau and most of the western United States. They average around three feet tall with males weighing over 250 pounds, while females weigh about half that. Named for their large burro-like ears, they are most active during dawn and dusk but can be found foraging at any time of day. One of their odd habits is that of "stotting" when alarmed, jumping sharply into the air and landing on all fours in lieu of running, quickly bouncing away from their enemies. Not shy of humans, they will eat

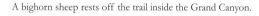

A bighorn sheep rests off the trail inside the Grand Canyon.

human food along with its packaging; this causes far too many to slowly die when their digestion system gets clogged with plastic. Please store your food to prevent animal access when in wilderness areas, and remember that it is illegal to feed any wild animal within national parks.

⚬**Pronghorn**: The fastest long-distance mammal on the face of the earth, pronghorns can run up to 65 miles per hour and maintain a speed of over 30 miles an hour for several miles. (Although a cheetah can hit a top speed over 70 miles per hour, it can only maintain its speed for about 250 yards.) Pronghorns are buff colored with a white belly and rump. Their namesake horns are small and insignificant in females, while the males' grow 10–12 inches long and have a longer and sharper point, curving back toward their rump with a shorter notch, or prong, that points forward. They average about three feet tall and four feet long, and can weigh 90–150 pounds. Pronghorn require wide open areas where they can run from any predator they spot with their extraordinary sight. Pronghorn populations were decimated during the late 1800s when their numbers decreased from over 35 million to only 13,000. Fast as they are, they cannot outrun a bullet. Due to federal protection, these animals now number about a quarter-million.

⚬**Bighorn Sheep**: Inhabiting rocky slopes, this sheep species can weigh up to 300 pounds; its horns alone can weigh 30 pounds. Amazing climbers, they use those skills regularly to escape predation. They are named for the male's large, curved horns, which they use to butt heads with other males in order to establish dominance. During these altercations, sometimes lasting up to 24 hours,

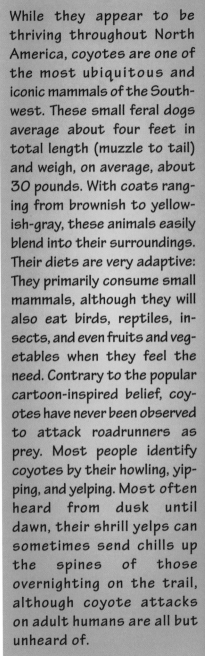

Side Step: Coyotes

While they appear to be thriving throughout North America, coyotes are one of the most ubiquitous and iconic mammals of the Southwest. These small feral dogs average about four feet in total length (muzzle to tail) and weigh, on average, about 30 pounds. With coats ranging from brownish to yellowish-gray, these animals easily blend into their surroundings. Their diets are very adaptive: They primarily consume small mammals, although they will also eat birds, reptiles, insects, and even fruits and vegetables when they feel the need. Contrary to the popular cartoon-inspired belief, coyotes have never been observed to attack roadrunners as prey. Most people identify coyotes by their howling, yipping, and yelping. Most often heard from dusk until dawn, their shrill yelps can sometimes send chills up the spines of those overnighting on the trail, although coyote attacks on adult humans are all but unheard of.

Red-tailed hawk (US Fish and Wildlife/Mark Bohn photo)

they charge each other at more than twenty miles an hour, cracking their horns together. It is reported that the sound can be heard over a mile away. Bighorns live in flocks of varying numbers, but they usually do not follow a single leader. Hunting, competition from domestic sheep herds, and disease all took their toll on bighorns, and they risked extinction during the early 1900s. Their numbers have stabilized but not substantially increased over time.

≈≈ Birds (nearly 300 species)

⚬Red-Tailed Hawk: Easily recognized by its distinctive screech (the one used in movie soundtracks no matter what eagle, hawk, or vulture is actually filmed) and its namesake tail, red-tails are the most common hawk in North America. Occupying nearly every habitat, they feed mostly on smaller mammals, but they will also eat snakes, carrion, and other birds. They typically nest in tall trees, cliff ledges, and any other place where they will have a commanding view of their territory. Other hawks inhabiting the plateau are the Cooper's hawk, the sharp-shinned hawk, and the goshawk.

⚬Common Raven: The smartest of all birds, ravens occur in all habitats over most of the Northern Hemisphere. Although often confused with crows, the raven is much larger, with a wingspan over 45 inches, a bigger "roman" beak, and a multitude of vocalizations. Ravens are very acrobatic in flight, diving, rolling, and doing somersaults, and sometimes they can even be seen playing catch with sticks in midair. Ubiquitous along the plateau, with their cacophonous calls and noisy "whooshing" wing beats, they seem to keep constant vigil of their landscape. Dangerous predators, they are opportunistic feeders of carrion, small animals, berries, eggs, beetles, human garbage, fish, and nearly everything in between. They are communal in nature and breeding pairs can be very territorial, regularly chasing off any hawk straying into their nesting area. In many areas of canyon country, ravens have become quite a nuisance, easily accessing food stored in soft-sided or Styrofoam coolers, packs, and cardboard boxes. In these areas, keep food and toiletries inside hard-sided containers or in your vehicle with the windows closed.

Broad-Tailed Hummingbird: Averaging four inches in length, broad-tails are actually longer than most hummers. The males are flashier than females, although they both have a green head and back and a white/buff underbelly. But the male's most distinctive feature is its throat, which is colored an iridescent red-pink. Their habitat includes most everything except high alpine and grassland areas, and they migrate annually to Central America for winters. One of the hummingbirds' unique features is their ability to enter a slower metabolic state called torpor on cold nights. Entering this altered condition allows them to maintain their body temperatures at about 55 degrees when air temperatures drop below 45 degrees. In flight, hummingbirds' wings beat about fifty times per second, and thus they require huge amounts of energy, which they receive mainly by consuming nectar from flowers, occasionally supplementing their diets with small spiders and insects.

California Condor: Condors, on the other hand, are the largest land bird in North America, with an amazing wingspan up to nine-and-a-half feet. These vultures are black with white patches on the underside of their wings, and a bald red or yellow/buff head. At this time, they are the rarest species of birds on the planet, and yet one of its longest-living with a lifespan up to 60 years. Considered extirpated in Arizona since 1924, this ugly but majestic species was reintroduced at the Vermilion Cliffs in 1996,

California condor
(NPS photo)

and as of 2012, there are about 73 condors riding the thermals around Grand Canyon and Zion national parks. They subsist on carrion, living off the carcass of most any mammal (and therefore subject to death from consuming lead ammo), but rarely eating reptiles or other birds. They can regularly go up to two weeks without a meal.

Western Bluebird: Both the male western bluebird and its cousin, the very slightly larger mountain bluebird, are a vivid blue. The western bluebird is usually a deeper blue and has a red-rust color on its shoulders and sometimes part of the back, while the mountain variety is more of a sky blue with no rust colored patches. Females of both species are more gray in color, with a slight pale blue tinge on their wings and tails. Western bluebirds forage for grasshoppers, beetles, and spiders, but they will also eat berries. Numbers of these brilliant birds are still decreasing in California and Arizona, as they prefer to nest in dead trees, which humans like to remove.

≋ Fish (over 40 species, 75 percent of these are non-native)

✿**Colorado River Cutthroat Trout**: This native trout can be found in river basins, preferring cool, clear water habitats along the plateau. The Colorado River cutthroat is considered one of the most beautiful fish in North America, with its brilliant golden color, black spots along its flanks and back, and pinkish-orange patches below its mouth and around its gills. This species is in extreme peril of extinction as it occupies only about 5 percent of its historic range. This is due to the stocking of non-native trout, and to loss of habitat as livestock grazing and various resource-extraction processes degrade water conditions.

A speckled dace
(US Fish and Wildlife/Paul Barrett photo)

✿**Speckled Dace**: These four-inch minnows are native to the West from Canada to Mexico. Along the plateau, the speckled dace is quite common and has adapted to many habitats, ranging from warm desert springs to cold, swift-flowing mountain streams. They are bottom feeders, usually consuming insect larvae, as well as fish eggs and algae. Their color is grayish green, usually with a darker stripe running along the sides, and shiny, silver-reflective scales. The dace's back is olive to brownish with darker blotches, or speckles, featured prominently along most of its body, save for its belly. Speckled dace have always been an important element of the ecosystem, yet five sub-species of this minnow are currently listed as endangered due to habitat destruction and the introduction of non-native species.

≋ Reptiles (over 35 species)

✿**Plateau Lizard**: This lizard is commonly found at lower elevations in brushy environments, as well as rock outcroppings and canyon walls. They average about 6 inches in total length, and their colors vary from gray to brown with dark side stripes. Males often have distinctive blue markings on their throat and belly. During territorial disagreements and in the mating season, males display their blue patches by executing an odd series of bobbing, bowing, and pushups, meant to impress the gals.

✿**Great Basin Gopher Snake**: If you see a snake anywhere along the plateau, nine times out of ten it will be a non-poisonous gopher snake. They live in a variety of ecosystems, and they move about at any time of day or night. Gopher snakes are great climbers and swimmers. Up

Harmless gopher snakes are often mistaken for rattlesnakes. Please do not harm them. (Mark Bratton/USAF photo)

to 6 feet in length, this species is buff to yellowish colored with dark, fairly uniform blotches along its body length, with smaller irregular blotches on its sides and a dark line between its eyes along the forehead. Gopher snakes kill their prey by constriction, eating mostly small rodents and birds. They can be very friendly, but people often will kill them simply because they resemble rattlesnakes. When provoked, they occasionally will hiss and shake their tails to mimic a rattler.

Woodhouse's toad (NPS/Randy Williams photo)

≋ **Amphibians** (over a dozen species)

☼**Woodhouse's Toad**: This toad is more active at night but commonly seen during the day. It is easily identified by the prominent white stripe down its back, while its body is warty and usually gray to yellow-brown in color. Growing up to 5 inches long, it will inhabit any area providing sufficient moisture. The male's most distinctive feature is its mating call that is reminiscent of a bawling calf. I call them "screaming baby toads." The call can be up to ten seconds long, in a trilling "wa-a-a-ah" sound produced from their ballooning vocal sac. Their warts and glands produce toxins, making them bad to eat—although they really do not cause warts in humans.

☼**Northern Leopard Frog**: These frogs were at one time the most widespread and abundant frogs in North America, but since the 1970s their numbers have been declining for reasons still unknown. They are a medium-sized frog, up to 4 inches long, with greenish-brown skins and irregular spots on their backs and legs. Lighter colored ridges adorn their sides, and their bellies are bright white. The female frogs are larger than the males. Living near permanent water sources, they will venture into heavy grasses to feed. These frogs are opportunistic carnivores and will eat almost anything that fits in their mouths including ants, worms, beetles, and even small frogs, snakes, and birds.

Mormon cricket (NPS/Don Arceneaux photo)

⚕ Spiders and Insects
(unknown number of species)

⚙ **Mormon Cricket**: About a half-inch to three-quarters of an inch in body length, Mormon Crickets can vary in color—brown, black, purple, red, or green. Although referred to as crickets, they are actually classified as katydids. These flightless insects can cover a mile a day while being limited to walking or hopping. At times, population explosions of Mormon crickets can produce swarms of millions, causing agricultural devastation. They earned their name from early pioneers when Salt Lake seagulls reportedly devoured hordes of these crickets, which had been destroying their first crop of wheat.

⚙ **Blue Copper Butterfly**: These very pretty bright to pastel blue butterflies have darker veins with lighter underwings; the females can be more brownish with darker spotting. They are small, with wingspans less than 1¼ inch, and they subsist mainly on flower nectar. Living at higher elevations in habitats of shrubs and brush, meadows and open forest, adults can be found "on wing" and flittering about from April to August.

⚙ **Tarantula**: These docile, splendid spiders have been reported at sizes up to 6 inches. Tarantulas have eight legs and are usually brown but can

also be black. They have hairy bodies and legs. They rarely bite, but when defending themselves, they can kick hairy bristles off their abdomens in the direction of their enemies. A small cloud of these bristles causes both physical and chemical harm to skin, and it can be fatal to small mammals if inhaled. Tarantula bites are not fatal, but people have died from infections that can subsequently set in, and from an anaphylactic reaction similar to a bee sting allergy. In late summer and autumn, male tarantulas can often be seen roaming in search of a potential mate.

Tarantulas are quite docile creatures (seen here with a close view of a Russian Thistle).

⁂ **Plants** (over 300 species)

⁂ **Trees**

✿**Coyote Willow**: Found almost exclusively in riparian habitats at elevations from 3,000–8,500 feet, these common willows can form thickets and grow up to 12 feet tall. Their narrow, long leaves, usually colored a grayish-green, are tapered at both ends. The flexible branches of this tree were used throughout centuries as building materials, for cordage, and to make magnificent baskets. Willows also produce salicin, a chemical close to aspirin, and indigenous people used this plant for various medicinal purposes. Coyote willow also plays an important role as forage for many animals.

✿**Aspen**: These tall, fast-growing, deciduous trees reach up to 85 feet in height. Their smooth bark is a light green-gray to white-gray, with black knots and irregular horizontal black lines. Aspens are the most widely distributed tree in North America from Alaska to Mexico, propagating via their root systems to form extensive groves referred to as "clonal colonies." Aspen are routinely called "quaking" or "trembling" aspens due to the appearance and sound of their leaves as they rustle in the wind. Native Americans and pioneers extracted a quinine substitute from the aspen's bark. The most vivid autumn colors in canyon country belong to aspens when they turn a brilliant orange.

✿**Pinyon Pine**: These evergreen conifers are a significant part of plateau woodlands, usually occurring at elevations of 4,500–7,500 feet in canyons, high plains, and foothills. They grow to 30 feet in an uneven,

◎ *Side Step*: Cryptobiotic Soils

These sporadic patches of living soil crust look like a thick, black, hairy mold or lichens in raised jagged mounds. They help fix nitrogen in the soil, aiding in the establishment of plants. They are extremely fragile, and if you happen to step on them it can take fifty years or more to repair the damage. So please, if you step off the trail for any reason, make sure you don't stomp on these vital building blocks of the desert soil. As the saying goes, "Don't bust the crust; tiptoe around the crypto."

Cryptobiotic soil with a pen for reference

spreading, slightly pyramid shape. The pinyon's 1- to 2-inch needles grow in pairs, and its 2-inch cones contain edible seeds measuring about a half-inch long. These sweet, fat rich pine nuts are still harvested by indigenous populations as they have been for centuries. For most people, pine nuts have a wonderful taste and texture, but some experience a phenomena first described in 2001, called "pine mouth," where eating pine nuts releases a bitter, metallic taste in the mouth. It was recently confirmed that a particular species from China has been causing the problem, not our native pinyons.

✿**Fremont Cottonwood**: Deciduous cottonwoods dominate riparian areas, growing up to 100 feet tall, with green, heart-shaped leaves that turn bright yellow in autumn. With age, their gray bark becomes deeply cracked and creviced. Native Americans used the bark and leaves to treat swelling, wounds, and headaches. They also chewed the inner bark to prevent scurvy. In late spring when cottonwood seeds mature, they are released in a flurry to waft on the breeze, each fluff of "cotton" carrying a tiny seed seeking the perfect conditions to germinate. On a warm breezy day, the cotton can fall to form little drifts that look like snow. Living up to 100 years, cottonwoods have a huge impact on their ecosystem by providing much-needed shade and nesting sites for birds and animals, also helping prevent soil erosion with their extensive root systems.

✿**Tamarisk**: Also known as salt cedars, tamarisks are non-native, invasive trees that suck water, strip nutrients, steal light, and thus wreak havoc on the native wildlife habitats. They can grow up to 20 feet tall in dense thickets, and have a reddish-brown bark that turns more purple with age. Their thin, scale-like leaves are gray-green and grow on spindly branches, the tips of which produce wispy masses of white or pink flowers any time from spring through fall. Introduced from southern Eurasia in the early 1800s to prevent soil erosion and still sold at nurseries for

A wonderful old cottonwood inside the Grand Canyon.

their delicate pink blooms, they spread rapidly through riparian areas. A few of the problems associated with this species include the displacement of native plants while providing paltry habitat of little nesting or food value, stream channel narrowing, and increased wildfire risk.

≈ Shrubs

⚘Four-Wing Saltbush: This species of saltbush is well adapted to different soil conditions and a wide range of temperatures, allowing it the widest distribution of any saltbush ranging from South Dakota to Mexico. These semi-evergreens (depending on climate) have gray-green leaves that grow about an inch in length with fine white hairs. They average about four feet high, but can get up to eight feet tall and fifteen feet in width. A boon to the ecosystem, this bush provides excellent cover for birds and small mammals, as well as providing food for a range of animals, with leaves high in total protein. The four "wings" in its name describe the paperlike, winged membrane that encapsulates its seeds. Indigenous peoples ground the seeds of four-wing saltbush into flour used in bread-making.

⚘Blackbrush: At elevations between 3,000 and 7,000 feet, blackbrush can form monocultures in large areas of dry, well-drained, sandy, gravelly, and rocky soils, where annual temperatures can range from 115 to minus 10 degrees. Blackbrush are short (3–4 feet) spiny-tipped plants with small, aromatic, gray-green, half-inch leaves, and small yellow flowers. In spring, its bark is ash gray, becoming darker with age and turning black when wet. These bushes provide browsing opportunities for many animals, but a chemical compound in new growth provides protection from heavy grazing.

⚘Mormon Tea: An interesting and somewhat common shrub, Mormon tea does not have leaves, per se, but photosynthesizes via its thin, jointed stems. Growing only 2–3 feet, its stems are bluish to bright green, each stem only a few inches long before it connects to its next stem with tiny, insignificant, brownish-black leaves in the connecting joints. Inconspicuous cone-like flowers turn brown as they dry. The botanical name for Mormon Tea is *ephedra*, the same drug used in decongestants and as a stimulant, and although this variety contains little ephedrine, if any, it has been used for centuries to treat stomach disorders, colds, fever, and headaches. (Before consuming any wild plant, make sure you know, absolutely, what that plant is and its specific use.)

✿**Big Sagebrush:** This classic range plant has the widest distribution of any shrub in North America, existing from Canada, south to Mexico, and east to Nebraska. Sagebrush is usually found at elevations from 4,000–10,000 feet, and can be found growing in large expanses along drier plains, desert woodlands, and rocky areas with deep enough soils. These evergreens average from 3–7 feet in height, and their leaves are small (less than 2 inches long). The gray-green leaves are covered with silvery hairs, and although they are loaded with protein, they contain a volatile oil making them unpalatable to cattle, but sheep will eat them in winter. Dense clustered stalks of tiny, pale yellow to cream-colored flowers grow on the ends of branches in late summer. Bad-tasting oils or not, wildlife thrives on sagebrush. It provides forage for insects, large and small mammals, and birds (including its heaviest user, the sage grouse), and provides nesting, protection, and escape cover. Unfortunately, big sagebrush currently covers about half of the territory it has in the past. Sage has a wonderfully pungent aroma similar to turpentine, and its sweet scent can permeate the air after a rainstorm.

✿**Russian Thistle**: Adored by singing cowboys, novelists, and moviemakers alike, the Russian thistle, or tumbleweed, is a historic icon that we who live here recognize as an invasive, noxious weed. Especially prolific in disturbed soil, this spiny annual bush can quickly grow up to three feet tall in the summer. It eventually breaks off from its stem and, when winds pick up enough, this weed quickly transforms into its more common namesake, the tumblin' tumbleweed. The rolling bushes effectively distribute seeds, which can number up to a quarter-million per plant. Russian thistle was first spotted in the United States in South Dakota in the late 1870s, reportedly mixed in with flaxseed brought in by Ukrainian farmers. Within thirty years it had spread to the California coast. The biggest problems associated with Russian thistle are the fire hazard it represents when the large dried heads accumulate, and the toxins that can build up in mature plants, harming foragers who may eat too much.

⚞ Wildflowers

✿**Plains Prickly Pear**: All true cacti, including prickly pears, are native only to the Americas. A few varieties of prickly pear cactus are indigenous to canyon country, but the low-growing plains species has the widest distribution, growing from Canada to Mexico at elevations from 4,000–10,000 feet. With green to greenish-blue oval pads averaging 3–4 inches, the prickly pear employs tiny, irritating barbed fibers called glochids at the base of longer spines to help protect it from foragers. Their moderate-sized flowers are usually yellow with tinges of red or sometimes magenta. The stunning blooms are easily desiccated by the sun and are short-lived unless they have partial shade or are lucky enough to blossom on a cloudy day. This cactus bears cylindrical one-inch fruit along the edge of the pad. Both the fruit and the pads are high in soluble fiber and provide food to a multitude of animals, especially when wildfire burns the spines off.

✿**Sego Lily**: This delicate plant has thin, grass-like leaves, green leafy stems, and beautiful flowers up to three inches across, comprised of three petals with three smaller "sepals" in between each petal. Petals are white and have purple-red blotches with yellow toward the center. Conspicuous in its simplicity, these early bloomers seem to thrive on dry, sandy soils. The sego lily is the state flower of Utah in honor of its edible bulb, which pioneers around Salt Lake Valley depended on for food during a long, cold winter in the mid-1800s. The bulb was usually roasted or boiled.

✿**Sacred Datura**: This plant bears one of the most easily identified flowers along the plateau, six-inch trumpet-shaped, white flowers scented in a light, sweet fragrance, blooming throughout the growing season. The plant itself can grow four to five feet across, and a few feet in height, with broad, rank-smelling dark green leaves with wavy edges that taper to a point. It is a member of the potato family, and as such, its flowers and leaves are poisonous. While this plant was used extensively by Native Americans in religious ceremonies, if not prepared correctly, its ingestion can be lethal.

All parts of the Sacred Datura contain enough poison to be lethal if ingested.

☼**Common Globemallow:** Growing in sandy soils and commonly seen along roadsides, globemallows have bright orange-red flowers that develop in clusters along two-foot stems in April and through the summer. Their green leaves resemble tiny maple leaves that are covered with gray-white, star-shaped hairs, giving them a sandpapery texture. The most drought tolerant of the mallows, it provides browse for bighorn sheep, pronghorn, and many other mammals. In wet springs globemallows (of which there are several species) can provide vivid orange displays, making them one of the showiest of the plateau wildflowers. Indigenous peoples used them to treat digestive disorders.

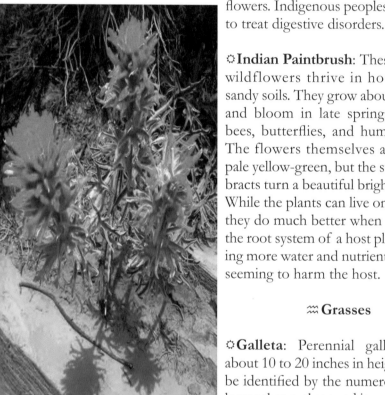

☼**Indian Paintbrush:** These vivid red wildflowers thrive in hot, dry, and sandy soils. They grow about a foot tall and bloom in late spring, attracting bees, butterflies, and hummingbirds. The flowers themselves are a rather pale yellow-green, but the surrounding bracts turn a beautiful bright red color. While the plants can live on their own, they do much better when attached to the root system of a host plant, obtaining more water and nutrients while not seeming to harm the host.

〜 **Grasses**

☼**Galleta:** Perennial galleta grows about 10 to 20 inches in height and can be identified by the numerous twisted leaves that curl around its main vertical spike. Its seed heads are purple to straw-colored spikelet clusters that

Indian Paintbrush is one of the most vividly colored wildflowers you'll see along the Colorado Plateau.

leave a zigzag pattern on the tip of its stalk after they have fallen off. Galleta occurs from 2,500–7,500 feet in a variety of soil conditions and is considered an important range grass with the ability to withstand heavy grazing, a necessary adaptation as it is desirable forage for a variety of mammals.

✿**Indian Ricegrass**: Indian ricegrass is another highly palatable browse plant for wild and domestic animals, and it is a key species in canyon country. It grows 10 to 30 inches tall, with several very thin sage-green leaves that grow from the base, rolling around the main stem. Seeds are black, protein rich, and are about half the size of a rice grain. Ricegrass is a relatively short-lived native perennial bunchgrass needing sandy well-drained soil. Beside its nutritional value, this grass also helps stabilize areas prone to wind erosion. Native Americans have used the seeds since Archaic times.

✿**Cheatgrass**: Also known as downy brome, this aggressive, invasive weed was introduced by ship to New York and is now a dominant grass along the Colorado Plateau. Cheatgrass averages around 18 inches, but can grow up to 30 inches in height. An annual bunchgrass, it has a drooping seed head with soft hairs covering the whole plant. As the 2- to 6-inch seed head matures it changes from a dark green with hints of purple to a straw color. The wedged seeds can be dispersed by wind, but if you ask me, they get around best by sticking to hikers' socks. Although tender new leaves make a good winter feed for grazers, when the grass dries out it can become injurious to an animal's mouth, eyes, ears, and feet. It gained its common name by "cheating" farmers of a vigorous wheat crop since it quickly establishes itself in vast areas, forcing out native grasses. This weed grass loves disturbed soil and has been known to produce over 10,000 plants per square yard. Its flammable nature makes it of prime concern during wildfire season.

Cheatgrass field with a close-up insert. If these seed heads get stuck to your shoes and socks please dispose of them properly to avoid spreading this noxious weed grass.

Chapter Six

Geology & Colored Canyons

A pile of rocks
ceases to be
a rock when
somebody
contemplates it
with the idea of a
cathedral in mind.

*Antoine
de
Saint-Exupery*

On this beautiful blue marble we call Earth, mountains, deserts, oceans, and continents are all continuously moving and changing. What makes the Colorado Plateau so unique is that it has long been a geologically stable region where you can actually view the history recorded in its eroded and exposed rock layers. Throughout much of its geologic history, what is now a plateau averaging 5,000 feet in elevation was actually close to sea levels. In this oxygen-rich environment, sediments like mud and sand turned brilliant colors when their iron content oxidized. Compacted by gravity and the ocean's weight, sedimentary layers eventually built up into harder rock surfaces. Due to the large rocky expanse and lack of moisture, less vegetation grows, and thus erosion has been the major force in unveiling these colorful rock formations.

The Castle at Capitol Reef is made primarily of Wingate Sandstone above with Chinle Formation below.

I would venture to say that, by and large, few people in the world have heard of the Colorado Plateau, and when most folks hear mention of "Colorado" they immediately think of the towering peaks of the Rockies. That said, most of those same folks would probably recognize many of the plateau's romantic scenes from popular media, having viewed these Western landscapes in movies and commercials during the course of their lives. This rock-dominated and surreal land can be spellbinding when its resplendently colored layers gleam in the sunset under darkening azure skies, and Hollywood knows it!

The Colorado Plateau is a land of incredible scenic beauty encompassing a huge part of the Four Corners region of Utah, Arizona, Colorado, and New Mexico. Its varied landforms lure thousands of visitors each year, and one of the first questions people will ask when viewing this fantastic landscape is, "How was it formed?"

I will attempt (attempt being the operative word here) to answer this question and explain, as best I can, how it all came about. What makes discussion of ancient geology difficult (besides my limited mental capacity and geologists' inevitable use of jargon), is the fact that, in many instances, when common sense would maintain that an area should contain certain rock layers, they are simply missing. With entire layers gone, scientists cannot explain if those layers were removed due to physical forces, or if they had never been deposited in the first place. And if they can't explain it, I'm not about to try. I'll just stick with the basics.

Creating the Land of the Sleeping Rainbow

Let's start at the deepest depths of the earth's crust. The earth is about 4.6 billion years old (4,600 million years), and both ocean crust and continental crust (land) float, if you will, on huge tectonic plates that are in constant motion above the earth's interior mantle. This crust formed when magma, under great heat and pressure, was eventually forced outward, cooling and condensing into large land masses. The tectonic plates shifting around the planet formed ancient islands and continents that collided with other land masses, at times creating singular supercontinents. Two of these supercontinents are Rodinia, occurring between 1,300 and 600 million years ago, and younger Pangea, existing between 360 and 245 million years ago.

Some 1.75 billion years ago the region we now call the Colorado Plateau was closer to the equator and was covered by an ancient ocean. The crust underlying the ocean's seabed is very different from the land forming continental crust. Oceanic crust is much thinner and denser, composed primarily of igneous mafic rocks (silicate minerals rich in magnesium and iron), the most common mafic rock being volcanic basalt. Continental crust, on the other hand, is thicker, less dense, and made up of all three classifications of rock. At its lower depths we find igneous (cooled magma) and metamorphic (transformed by pressure and temperature) rocks, and higher up there are sedimentary formations (deposits of eroded rock subjected to compaction or cementation). The depths of the continental foundations are mostly made up of metamorphic schist and gneiss, along with igneous quartz and granite, ranging in age from 1,950 to 1,700 million years old.

The story of the Colorado Plateau begins when areas of continental crust had already been created, and suddenly (in geologic time), during the Early Proterozoic era, a volcanic chain of islands formed and subsequently drifted toward what is now North America. This volcanic chain eventually collided with North America's continental shores, folding and attaching these basement rocks to the continent. Ancient mountains, born from these opposing land masses and other volcanic events, would be built up and then worn down flat on many occasions throughout the earth's ancient history. Nowadays, these schist and granite rocks dominate the foundation of the plateau, although they are rarely seen. Only in the deepest depths of such chasms as the Grand Canyon can they actually be viewed.

The oldest sedimentary rocks, such as sandstone, limestone, and mudstone, were formed as the basement rocks were uplifted, exposed,

Some of the oldest exposed rocks on earth can be found by the Colorado River inside Grand Canyon.

The lines of fractured rock in the wash along Druid Arch Trail will someday form fins similar to those in the background.

and eroded. These deposits accumulated in a shallow marine basin that encroached from the west during the time of the ancient supercontinent Rodinia. During the Late Proterozoic era, rifts began to form in Rodinia's vast surface, and North America split away from what are now Asia, Australia, and Antarctica.

The dawning of the Paleozoic era saw the plateau region repeatedly inundated, primarily from the southwest, by tropical oceans. From this time and through the Mesozoic period, the plateau remained at, below, or near sea level. The Ancient Rocky Mountains rose along the eastern margins of the plateau, and erosive effects whisked sediments along rivers and floodplains, depositing them onto the lowlands. Alternating layers of sedimentary rocks were laid down including: limestone (primarily calcite containing an accumulation of shells, corals, and other organic debris), sandstone (sandy composites), siltstone (sand and clay composite), and shale (solidified mud or clay that fractures in sheets). This era also witnessed the most widespread and rapid explosion of life in earth's history, with widespread varieties of fish, reptiles, and amphibians evolving at this time.

As previously mentioned, it was in this oxygen-rich world of shallow seas that these sediments turned vivid colors as their iron content was oxidized. When the seas retreated, layers could either be carried away by erosion or built up by stream deposits and dune creation. Layers of marine sediments accumulated for over 300 million years, and it wasn't until the formation of the next major supercontinent, Pangea, and its coinciding upheavals that dry, land-based deposits began to dominate. It was during this time frame, the Late Paleozoic era, as the dry environment evaporated salt water from the sedimentary layers, that the Paradox Basin was formed, encompassing a vast portion of the plateau. The contradiction of this basin is its dry, evaporative nature, containing sediments from recurrent cycles of both deep and shallow oceans, in contrast to other Rocky Mountain basins.

The Paleozoic era ended in an anomaly (referred to geologically as an unconformity), where the sedimentary history is either missing or did not happen. During this same relative time, the mother of all mass extinctions occurred, the Permian-Triassic Event, when over 95 percent of all marine species and 70 percent of land animals went extinct for unknown reasons, although a combination of environmental changes and a major catastrophic event has been suggested as the possible culprit. This was the third and largest mass extinction event recorded in Earth's history.

The dawn of the age of reptiles was ushered in during the Mesozoic era. Huge volcanic eruptions occurred as Pangea began to fragment, slowly drifting into the separate landmasses we now recognize as the seven continents. A hot, dry North America drifted westward, pressing against oceanic plates, and the region was elevated above sea level. Simultaneously, the Ancestral Rockies were still eroding and leaving large terrestrial deposits that were subsequently river swept and windblown into an extensive accumulation of sand dunes, ultimately hardening into sandstone. Volcanic activity also made its mark on the geology of the middle Jurassic period as pyroclastic ash was widely dispersed across the plateau, and other mass die-offs (mostly of marine life) were recorded. Dinosaurs slowly began to claim dominance at this time, and the first true mammals evolved while the planet got cooler and wetter and Pangea began to drift apart.

During the Cretaceous period, the plateau became increasingly wetter and more humid. Land around present-day Nevada was uplifted, providing more sediment as an interior seaway coming in from the east flooded most of the region. This period marked the end of the Mesozoic era with another mass extinction, which ended the reign of the dinosaur. This episode of extinction, the Cretaceous-Paleogene Event, may have been caused by one or more catastrophic events, or possibly by the various volcanic activities that were happening at this same time. The sea finally retreated for the last time and left the area primed for rock sculpting.

What geologists seem to find most intriguing about the plateau is that it has remained remarkably stable during the last 600 million years. To the north and east, volcanic activity and mountain building pushed areas ever higher. To the west and south, the earth was being stretched into the Basin and Range Province, characterized by a multitude of elongated faulted mountain chains alternating with flat arid valleys in between. As the seas retreated, both the Rockies and the Colorado Plateau were pushed up through their former basement foundations. For reasons not yet known, the plateau managed to maintain itself as a single tectonic mass, eventually rising over a half-mile above the Basin and Range. Rivers began to flow to the southwest, and a great drainage system was formed.

Just over 5 million years ago, a system of deepening canyons was slowly carved into the plateau, carrying tons of sediment down toward the predominant waterway of the region, the mighty Colorado River. It is this natural power of erosion that exposed spectacularly colorful rock layers century by century, making the Colorado Plateau a visual treat that the Native Americans referred to as the "The Land of the Sleeping Rainbow."

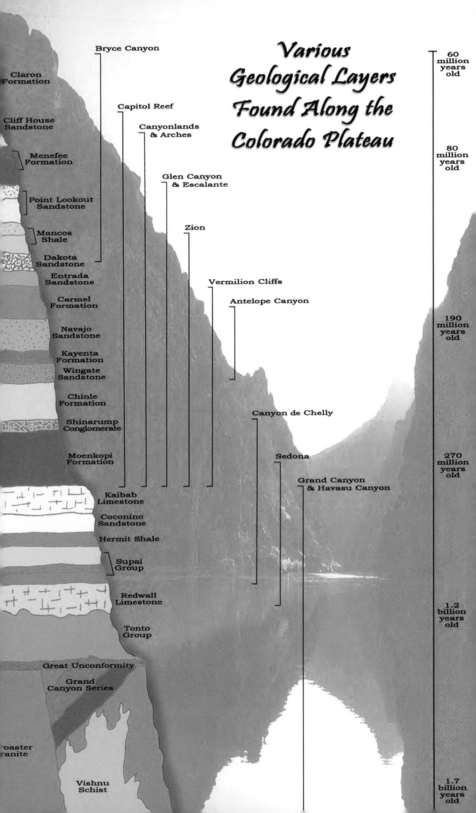

Various Geological Layers Found Along the Colorado Plateau

General List of the Geological Rock Layers Found Along the Colorado Plateau

Claron Formation: The Claron Formation is the predominantly limestone layer that produced the fantastic hoodoos of Bryce Canyon and Cedar Breaks. About 60 million years ago, a large area of the plateau was covered by Lake Claron, a huge water mass that enveloped nearly 18,000 square miles. Sediments and algae settling in the lake's bottom formed a pasty silt that cemented these sediments together. This highly colored stratum of pink, orange, and red formed Bryce's fantastic features as ice and rain wore away at the weak sedimentary limestone. The colors are the result of various amounts of oxidizing iron. Surprisingly, there is an absence of fossils surviving from this time.

Cliff House Sandstone: This orange-buff colored sandstone layer, containing very few fossils, formed as sand was deposited from an episode of advancing sea. This formation produced a preponderance of alcoves that made wonderful, and often used, natural shelters for many ancestral peoples.

Menefee Formation: A swampy, flat coastal plain formed over 80 million years ago and resulted in the dark brown and blackish colored shale made from organic decay. This formation can also contain sandstone and coal seams.

Point Lookout Sandstone: A retreating sea formed this layer of buff-colored sandstone as the shallow water changed the deposits from shale back to sandstone beach deposits. Although this layer contained many small alcoves, it appears they were not utilized by indigenous people. Very few fossils occur in this deposit.

Mancos Shale: Grayish in color, these shale deposits are made from organic materials and fine particles. Many fossils have been found in this layer, including clams, snails, oysters, and ammonites.

Dakota Sandstone: This light-colored, coarse-grained sandy deposit has shallow-marine elements and occasional mudflat sediments.

Entrada Sandstone: Formed when windblown sediments settled in still water, this layer is most often a light orange, but can be red or cream colored. Containing scant fossil deposits, this sandstone formed the magnificent arches of Arches National Park.

The fantastic hoodoos of Bryce Canyon are predominantly made of Claron Formation limestone.

Carmel Formation: This brownish-red layer is made from a mixture of limestone and siltstone deposited along a retreating sea. This formation contains bivalve and ammonite fossils similar to those found in the Mancos layer.

Navajo Sandstone: Forming vertical walls with round cliff tops, these deposits were made during a time of intense winds and huge drifting deserts. They range in color from brown to nearly white. The fossil history for this layer is poor but does contain a record of giant stromatolites.

Kayenta Formation: These layers, from sandy stream deposits, are typically red to brown and tend to form ledges and cliff bands.

Wingate Sandstone: Deposited in a similar manner as Navajo Sandstone, the Wingate's color usually runs red to pale orange. Combined, these three layers, the Wingate, Kayenta, and Navajo formations can form sheer vertical cliffs over 2,000 feet tall.

Chinle Formation: This layer is colored from red and brown to gray, green, yellow, and even the occasional light bluish-purple. Streams deposited this layer containing mud, silt, and volcanic ash. This formation includes the **Shinarump Conglomerate**, made of pebbles and stones called "clasts," cemented together with smaller particles. Good examples of the Chinle Formation can be found in the Painted Desert.

Moenkopi Formation: This red to dark brown layer creates steep slopes and vertical walls. It was collected in mudflats and tidal pools from stream-born silt and contains a great number of ripples and channel deposits.

Kaibab Limestone: The youngest of the Grand Canyon formations, this creamy yellow layer forms the upper rim of the canyon. It

---

Side Step: Arches Defined

Among the most prominent geological features of the Colorado Plateau are its numerous arches. In other parts of the country, visitors may seek out waterfalls or lakes, but in the land of eroded sedimentary rock, multitudes of tourists hike high and low to see as many natural arches as possible. An arch is any rock exposure where a hole has naturally formed, leaving an intact frame. A three-foot opening is the minimum size to be considered an official arch. These definitions are somewhat arbitrary, since there are also many natural bridges in the region that are not considered true arches since the opening has been formed primarily due to a river or creek undercutting the rock strata. The largest concentration of natural arches in the world can be found at the aptly named Arches National Park, which contains over two thousand of these marvelous geologic features.

Delicate Arch

contains fossils of fish, corals, sponges, and other life forms that lived and developed in a shallow, warm marine environment about 270 million years ago. It has eroded into ledgy cliffs.

☐ **Coconino Sandstone:** This formation is basically petrified sand dunes and is mainly comprised of quartz sand. Though little or no skeletal fossils remain, a number of reptile footprints have been found pressed into this white- to cream-colored layer.

☐ **Hermit Shale:** This crumbly and easily eroded layer is colored a deep, rusty red. Due to its erosive characteristics, this shale tends to undermine the limestone and sandstone rocks that rest above it, causing huge blocks to break off, many of which can be seen near Grand Canyon's Tonto Trail.

 Side Step : Keeping Track of Geologic Time

Geologists use a seemingly convoluted time scale, and it can be difficult to keep track of its eons and eras. I've included this little bit of information to see if I can put it into some kind of order for you (and for me too). First of all, the oldest time frame was the Precambrian Eon, which began 4.6 billion years ago when the earth was formed. It has been divided into three *eras*, the Hadrean, the Archean, and the Proterozoic. The Precambrian Eon takes in nearly 90 percent of the entire history of the earth and lasted all the way up to 545 million years ago. Scientists then divided the history of Earth's geologic times into many distinct eras of time. For our purposes these blocks of time are commonly referred to as the Proterozoic or Precambrian (before life — as in bacteria, from 4.6 billion to 545 million years ago), the Paleozoic (early life — mostly fish and simple aquatic creatures, 545–250 m.y.a.), the Mesozoic (middle life —think dinosaurs, 250 – 65 m.y.a.), and the Cenozoic (late life —mammals, 65 m.y.a. – present).

Okay so far? Well, let's continue since there is also another geologic timeline which overlaps the previous, further defining and classifying each era into a series of periods. After the Precambrian Eon, these periods are, in ascending order, the Cambrian (545–500 million years ago), the Devonian (500–410 m.y.a.), the Mississipian (410–300 m.y.a.), the Pennsylvanian (300– 290 m.y.a.), the Permian (290–250 m.y.a.), the Triassic (250–200 m.y.a.), the Jurassic (200–150 m.y.a.), the Tertiary (65–2 m.y.a.), and the Quarternary (2 m.y.a.– present). It's not confusing at all, is it?

Supai Formation: This formation is actually made up of four distinct layers. In the Grand Canyon, this stacked collection of shales and sandstones looks like a huge staircase of alternating ledges and slopes. While western sections of this layer contain marine fossils, the eastern sections contain plentiful plant life and footprints of reptiles and amphibians. Generally speaking, the shale is bright red in color with sandstone caps of tan.

Redwall Limestone: The cliff-forming Redwall was laid down during the time of a retreating shallow sea. It is composed of gray dolomite (calcium magnesium carbonate) and blue-gray to dark brown limestone with white chert (ultra-fine quartz crystals). The surface of this layer actually gets its red

The Mittens in Monument Valley contain four distinct layers, Organ Rock shale, de Chelly sandstone, and Moenkopi shale topped with Shinarump siltstone.

color from the iron-rich Supai and Hermit formations dripping on it.

Tonto Group: This grouping, containing trilobite fossils, occurred as the ocean returned to the area and moved toward the east. It includes Tapeats Sandstone (coarse-grained sand and conglomerate of a dark brown color), Bright Angel Shale (off-shore mud deposits, usually green in color), and Muav Limestone (deposited further off-shore, and gray in color).

Great Unconformity Gap: There is a break in the geologic record where rocks below the Tonto Group are missing from the sequence.

Grand Canyon Supergroup: This formation, eroded away from most of Grand Canyon, is comprised of nine geologic formations laid down by a great shallow sea that extended all the way to Lake Superior. The Supergroup is divided into three sections, the Unkar Group, the Nankoweap Formation, and the Chuar Group. The only sign of life in this layer are fossils of primitive algae.

Vishnu Schist and Zoroaster Granite: This dark grey or black layer contains metamorphic and igneous rocks formed deep below the earth's surface. No identifiable fossils have been found in this, the most ancient exposed layer of rock.

"It's good to have an end to journey toward but it is the journey that matters, in the end." *Ursula Le Guin*

Index

"Each journey begins and ends. Life is such a journey, yet it is full of journeys within." *Chinese proverb*